SPARKNOTES™

101

Sociology

SPARK PUBLISHING

Copyright © 2006 by Spark Publishing

SPARKNOTES is a registered trademark of SparkNotes LLC

Spark Publishing
120 Fifth Avenue
New York, NY 10011
www.sparknotes.com

ISBN-10: 1-4114-0333-9
ISBN-13: 978-1-4114-0333-8

Please submit all changes or report errors to www.sparknotes.com/errors

Printed and bound in the United States.

Library of Congress Cataloging-in-Publication Data

Sparknotes 101 sociology.
    p. cm.
    Includes index.
    ISBN 1-4114-0333-9
    1. Sociology—Textbooks. I. SparkNotes LLC. II. Title: SparkNotes one hundred one sociology. III. Title: SparkNotes one hundred and one sociology. IV. Title: One hundred one sociology. V. Title: One hundred and one sociology.
HM586.S645 2005
301—dc22
                                2005019417

Contents

Acknowledgments

SparkNotes would like to thank the following writers and contributors:

Carol Apt, Ph.D.
Associate Professor, Department of Sociology
South Carolina State University

Thao L. Ha
Teaching Assistant, Department of Sociology
University of Texas at Austin

Christina Myers, Ph.D.
Associate Professor, Department of Sociology and Anthropology
Emporia State University

El Rayah A. Osman, Ph.D.
Associate Professor, Department of Sociology
South Carolina State University

Anaxos, Inc.

A Note from SparkNotes

Welcome to the *SparkNotes 101* series! This book will help you succeed in your introductory college course for sociology.

Every component of this study guide has been designed to help you process the material more quickly and score higher on your exams. You'll see lots of headings, lists, charts, and, most important, no long blocks of text. This format will allow you to quickly situate yourself and easily get to the crux of your course.

We've included these features to help you get the most out of this book:

Introduction: Before diving in to the major chapters, you may want to get a broader view of the field of sociology. The Introduction will discuss the beginnings of sociology as an academic discipline, the related social sciences, and some possible career paths for students interested in pursuing further studies.

Chapters 1–7: Each chapter provides clarification of material included in your textbook. Key features include:

- **Shaded text boxes:** Throughout the text, these call out main points and provide related information.

- **Examples:** These clarify main points and show you how sociological concepts play out in the real world.

- **Key Terms:** Important sociological terms are bolded throughout each chapter for quick scanning and reviewing. Definitions for these terms are compiled in the glossary at the back of the book.

- **Chapter Summary:** This end-of-chapter summary provides an at-a-glance recap of major topics and ideas.

- **Sample Test Questions:** Ten study questions, both short answer and multiple choice, show you the kind of questions you are most likely to encounter on a test and give you the chance to practice what you've learned. Answers are provided.

Major Figures: This section provides a summary of the major figures presented in the chapters, along with their significance. Names of major figures are bolded in each chapter.

Glossary: Review new terms and refresh your memory at exam time with the glossary at the end of the book.

Index: Use the index to make navigation easier or to look up specific concepts, terms, and people.

You'll notice that this book has only seven chapters, while your textbook might have twenty or more. Not to worry—it's all here. We've gone for concision to make your studying easier. We've organized the material in a clear, logical way that won't over-whelm you—but *will* give you everything you need to know to keep up in class.

We hope *SparkNotes 101: Sociology* helps you, gives you confi-dence, and occasionally saves your butt! Your input makes us better. Let us know what you think or how we can improve this book at **www.sparknotes.com/comments**.

Introduction

Sociology is the systematic and scientific study of human social life. Sociologists study people as they form groups and interact with one another. The groups they study may be small, such as married couples, or large, such as a subculture of suburban teenagers. Sociology places special emphasis on studying societies, both as individual entities and as elements of a global perspective.

The Birth of Sociology

Auguste Comte (1798–1857), widely considered the "father of sociology," became interested in studying society because of the changes that took place as a result of the French Revolution and the Industrial Revolution. During the French Revolution, which began in 1789, France's class system changed dramatically. Aristocrats suddenly lost their money and status, while peasants, who had been at the bottom of the social ladder, rose to more powerful and influential positions. The Industrial Revolution followed on the heels of the French Revolution, unfolding in Western Europe throughout the 1800s. During the Industrial Revolution, people abandoned a life of agriculture and moved to cities to find factory jobs. They worked long hours in dangerous conditions for low pay. New social problems emerged and, for many decades, little was done to address the plight of the urban poor.

Comte looked at the extensive changes brought about by the French Revolution and the Industrial Revolution and tried to make sense of them. He felt that the social sciences that existed at the time, including political science and history, couldn't adequately explain the chaos and upheaval he saw around him. He decided an entirely new science was needed. He called this new science *sociology*, which comes from the root word *socius*, a Latin word that means "companion" or "being with others."

Comte decided that to understand society, one had to follow certain procedures, which we know now as the **scientific method**. The scientific method is the use of systematic and specific procedures to test theories in psychology, the natural sciences, and other fields. Comte also believed in **positivism**, which is the application of the scientific method to the analysis of society. Comte felt that sociology could be used to inspire social reforms and generally make a society a better place for its members. Comte's standards of "research" were not nearly as exacting as today's, and most of his conclusions have been disregarded, as they were based mostly on observation rather than serious investigation.

In the United States, sociology was first taught as an academic discipline at the University of Kansas in 1890, at the University of Chicago in 1892, and at Atlanta University in 1897. Over time, it spread to other universities in North America. The first department of sociology opened at McGill University in Montreal, Canada, in 1922, followed by sociology departments at Harvard University in 1930 and at the University of California at Berkeley in the 1950s.

Types of Sociology

Not all universities approach sociology the same way, and the new science evolved differently depending on where it was taught and who was teaching it. The two major types of sociology that emerged were **qualitative sociology** and **quantitative sociology**. Today, most universities use both qualitative and quantitative methods of inquiry, and one method is not necessarily better than the other.

QUALITATIVE SOCIOLOGY

At the University of Chicago, **Albion Small** (1854–1926) developed **qualitative sociology**, which is concerned mainly with trying to obtain an accurate picture of a group and how it operates in the world. Small and his followers were particularly interested in understanding how immigration was affecting the city and its residents. From the middle of the nineteenth century to roughly the middle of the twentieth century, massive numbers of people immigrated to the United States from a variety of countries. Chicago in particular attracted many immigrants from Poland.

Early sociologists were fascinated by the social changes they saw taking place and began conducting qualitative studies that involved personal interviews and observations of ethnic rituals and ceremonies.

Some University of Chicago sociologists actually went back to Poland to interview people who were about to immigrate to the United States, who had relatives who were immigrants, or who had no intention of immigrating anywhere. In keeping with the spirit of qualitative sociology, the researchers felt that they could understand the experiences of Polish immigrants only if they also understood their reality and experiences before they left their homeland.

Today, qualitative sociology emphasizes understanding individuals' experiences by examining their books, television programs, interactions, and ceremonies, among other elements. For example, a sociologist hoping to understand the experiences of emergency medical technicians (EMTs) might spend time riding in the backs of ambulances as the EMTs go out on calls.

QUANTITATIVE SOCIOLOGY

Sociology at Harvard University developed differently. Like the University of Chicago sociologists, Harvard sociologists wanted to understand the immigrant experience, but they went about their research in a quantitative way. **Quantitative sociology** relies on statistical analysis to understand experiences and trends. While some researchers at Harvard did talk to people and observe them, many preferred to remain within the confines of the university and quantify their data to render it suitable for statistical manipulation.

The Other Social Sciences

Social sciences concern people's relationships and interactions with one another. Sociology, with its emphasis on social life, falls into this category. A multidisciplinary field, sociology draws from a variety of other social sciences, including anthropology, political science, psychology, and economics.

ANTHROPOLOGY

Anthropology concerns individual cultures in a society, rather than the society as a whole. Traditionally, it focuses on what might be termed "primitive" cultures, such as the Yanomamo people of the South American jungle, who live much the same way they did hundreds of years ago. Anthropologists place special emphasis on language, kinship patterns, and cultural artifacts.

POLITICAL SCIENCE

Political science concerns the governments of various societies. It considers what kind of government a society has, how it formed, and how individuals attain positions of power within a particular government. Political science also concerns the relation of people in a society to whatever form of government they have.

PSYCHOLOGY

Psychology takes the individual out of his or her social circumstances and examines the mental processes that occur within that person. Psychologists study the human brain and how it functions, considering issues such as memory, dreams, learning, and perception.

ECONOMICS

Economics focuses on the production and distribution of society's goods and services. Economists study why a society chooses to produce what it does, how money is exchanged, and how people interact and cooperate to produce goods.

What Sociologists Do

People with training in sociology pursue a variety of different career and research paths. Because "society" is such a broad field of study, a background in sociology helps support dozens of different career choices. What follows are several broad areas in which sociologists frequently choose to apply their skills and interests.

SOCIAL WELFARE

Some people pursue degrees in sociology because they want to change society for the better. They study problems such as poverty, prejudice, and world hunger and attempt to find solutions. Jobs that relate to these kinds of interests include:

- Social worker
- Child welfare worker
- Adoption agency worker
- Foreign aid worker
- Peace Corps/VISTA volunteer
- Clergy

CRIME AND DEVIANCE

Many sociologists focus their research on understanding the roots of criminal and deviant behavior. Sociologists who focus on crime and deviance may conduct studies of juvenile delinquents, female criminals, or other subgroups of offenders. A background in this type of sociology prepares people for careers such as:

- Law enforcement officer
- Attorney
- Prison administrator

HEALTHCARE

An understanding of changing demographics and culture is essential for keeping members of a society healthy. Some sociologists apply their knowledge to the field of healthcare. They might take the following kinds of jobs:

- Doctor
- Psychiatrist
- Marriage or family counselor

INTERNATIONAL RELATIONS AND DIPLOMACY

Maintaining good relations with other societies is always important. Sociologists who specialize in international relations must understand the intricacies of how their society interacts with others. Interest in international relations might lead to such jobs as:

- Diplomat
- Public relations representative
- Government communications worker

EDUCATION

Many people study sociology because they want to develop more effective ways to educate a society's youth or because they want to continue learning and teaching about sociology itself. Such people might hold the following types of jobs:

- K-12 teacher
- College professor
- Educational policy-maker

＊　　＊　　＊　　＊　　＊　　＊　　＊　　＊

It's important to note the difference between sociology and social work. Social work is an **applied science**, since it is designed to solve a specific problem in a particular setting. Social work takes the principles found in sociology and applies them to a particular issue. For example, current sociological research indicates that men are more likely than women to commit suicide and that white people are more likely to take their own lives than black people. A social worker might take that knowledge and apply it to the real world by tailoring suicide-prevention programs to focus on the needs of white males.

This list covers just a handful of the possible directions your studies in sociology may take you. As you'll learn throughout your sociology course, a thorough understanding of the workings of society is applicable to an endless number of career paths.

Society and Culture

- What Is a Society?
- Types of Societies
- Norms
- Status and Roles
- Culture
- Hierarchy of Cultures
- The Interaction of Cultures

The society in which we live determines everything from the food we eat to the choices we make. The word *society* comes from the latin root *socius*, meaning "companion" or "being with others." A society consists of people who share a territory, who interact with each other, and who share a culture. Some societies are, in fact, groups of people united by friendship or common interests. Our respective societies teach us how to behave, what to believe, and how we'll be punished if we don't follow the laws or customs in place.

Sociologists study the way people learn about their own society's cultures and how they discover their place within those cultures. They also examine the ways in which people from differing cultures interact and sometimes clash—and how mutual understanding and respect might be reached.

What Is a Society?

According to sociologists, a **society** is a group of people with common territory, interaction, and culture. **Social groups** consist of two or more people who interact and identify with one another.

- **Territory:** Most countries have formal boundaries and territory that the world recognizes as theirs. However, a society's boundaries don't have to be geopolitical borders, such as the one between the United States and Canada. Instead, members of a society, as well as nonmembers, must recognize particular land as belonging to that society.

  > EXAMPLE: *The society of the Yanomamo has fluid but definable land boundaries. Located in a South American rain forest, Yanamamo territory extends along the border of Brazil and Venezuela. While outsiders would have a hard time determining where Yanomamo land begins and ends, the Yanomamo and their neighbors have no trouble discerning which land is theirs and which is not.*

- **Interaction:** Members of a society must come in contact with one another. If a group of people within a country has no regular contact with another group, those groups cannot be considered part of the same society. Geographic distance and language barriers can separate societies within a country.

  > EXAMPLE: *When India won independence from Great Britain in 1947, Muslim Indians seeking to establish a predominantly Muslim state created East and West Pakistan. These two regions were separated by thousands of miles across the northern part of India. Soon, it became apparent that the lack of interaction between East and West Pakistan was making it difficult to establish and maintain a unified society.*

Although Islam was practiced in both parts of the country, the residents of East Pakistan spoke Bengali, while the residents of West Pakistan spoke Urdu. Geographic distance, language differences, and other factors proved insurmountable. In 1971, the nation split into two countries, with West Pakistan assuming the name Pakistan *and East Pakistan becoming* Bangladesh. *Within each newly formed society, people had a common culture, history, and language, and distance was no longer a factor.*

- **Culture:** People of the same society share aspects of their culture, such as language or beliefs. **Culture** refers to the language, values, beliefs, behavior, and material objects that constitute a people's way of life. It is a defining element of society.

  EXAMPLE: Some features of American culture are the English language, a democratic system of government, cuisine (such as hamburgers and corn on the cob), and a belief in individualism and freedom.

PLURALISM

The United States is a society composed of many groups of people, some of whom originally belonged to other societies. Sociologists consider the United States a **pluralistic society**, meaning it is built of many groups. As societies modernize, they attract people from countries where there may be economic hardship, political unrest, or religious persecution. Since the industrialized countries of the West were the first to modernize, these countries tend to be more pluralistic than countries in other parts of the world.

Many people came to the United States between the mid-nineteenth and mid-twentieth centuries. Fleeing poverty and religious persecution, these immigrants arrived in waves from Europe and Asia and helped create the pluralism that makes the United States unique.

Pluralism in the Neighborhood Both cities and regions reflect pluralism in the United States. Most major American cities have areas in which people from particular backgrounds are concentrated, such as Little Italy in New York, Chinatown in San Francisco, and Little Havana in Miami. Regionally, people of Mexican descent tend to live in those states that border Mexico. Individuals of Cuban descent are concentrated in Florida. Spanish-speaking people from other Caribbean islands, such as Puerto Rico and the Dominican Republic, are more likely to live in the Northeast.

Assimilation

Some practices that are common in other societies will inevitably offend or contradict the values and beliefs of the new society. Groups seeking to become part of a pluralistic society often have to give up many of their original traditions in order to fit in—a process known as **assimilation**.

> EXAMPLE: *When people arrive in the United States from other countries, they most likely speak a foreign language. As they live here, they generally learn at least some English, and many become fluent. Their children are most likely bilingual, speaking English as well as the language of their parents. By the third generation, the language originally spoken by their grandparents is often lost.*

In pluralistic societies, groups do not have to give up all of their former beliefs and practices. Many groups within a pluralistic society retain their ethnic traditions.

> EXAMPLE: *Although Chinese immigrants started arriving in the United States 150 years ago, Chinese-American communities still follow some traditions, such as celebrating the Lunar New Year.*

Melting Pot? *The United States is commonly referred to as a* **melting pot**, *a society in which people from different societies blend together into a single mass. Some sociologists prefer the term "multicultural," pointing out that even if a group has been in this country for many generations, they probably still retain some of their original heritage. The term* **"multiculturalism"** *recognizes the original heritages of millions of Americans, noting that Americans who are originally from other societies do not necessarily have to lose their individual markers by melting into the mainstream.*

Equality

In a truly pluralistic society, no one group is officially considered more influential than another. In keeping with this belief, the United States does not, for example, put a legal quota on how many Italian Americans can vote in national elections, how many African Americans may run for public office, or how many Vietnamese Americans can live on a certain street. However, powerful informal mechanisms, such as prejudice and discrimination, work to keep many groups out of the political process or out of certain neighborhoods.

Types of Societies

The society we live in did not spring up overnight; human societies have evolved slowly over many millennia. However, throughout history, technological developments have sometimes brought about dramatic change that has propelled human society into its next age.

Social Revolutions

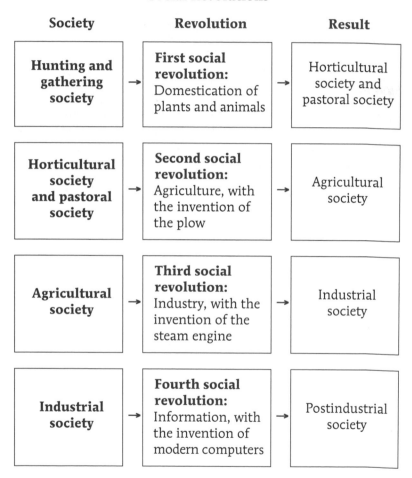

Society	Revolution	Result
Hunting and gathering society →	**First social revolution:** Domestication of plants and animals →	Horticultural society and pastoral society
Horticultural society and pastoral society →	**Second social revolution:** Agriculture, with the invention of the plow →	Agricultural society
Agricultural society →	**Third social revolution:** Industry, with the invention of the steam engine →	Industrial society
Industrial society →	**Fourth social revolution:** Information, with the invention of modern computers →	Postindustrial society

HUNTING AND GATHERING SOCIETIES

Hunting and gathering societies survive by hunting game and gathering edible plants. Until about 12,000 years ago, all societies were hunting and gathering societies.

There are five basic characteristics of hunting and gathering societies:

1. The primary institution is the family, which decides how food is to be shared and how children are to be socialized, and which provides for the protection of its members.
2. They tend to be small, with fewer than fifty members.
3. They tend to be nomadic, moving to new areas when the current food supply in a given area has been exhausted.
4. Members display a high level of interdependence.
5. Labor division is based on sex: men hunt, and women gather.

The **first social revolution**—the domestication of plants and animals—led to the birth of the horticultural and pastoral societies.

Twilight of the Hunter-Gatherers Hunting and gathering societies are slowly disappearing, as the encroachment of civilization destroys the land they depend on. The Pygmies in Africa are one of the few remaining such societies.

HORTICULTURAL SOCIETIES

In a **horticultural society**, hand tools are used to tend crops. The first horticultural societies sprang up about 10,000–12,000 years ago in the most fertile areas of the Middle East, Latin America, and Asia. The tools they used were simple: sticks or hoe-like instruments used to punch holes in the ground so that crops could be planted. With the advent of horticultural machinery, people no longer had to depend on the gathering of edible plants—they could now grow their own food. They no longer had to leave an area when the food supply was exhausted, as they could stay in one place until the soil was depleted.

PASTORAL SOCIETIES

A **pastoral society** relies on the domestication and breeding of animals for food. Some geographic regions, such as the desert regions of North Africa, cannot support crops, so these societies learned how to domesticate and breed animals. The members of a pastoral society must move only when the grazing land ceases to be usable. Many pastoral societies still exist in Africa, Latin America, and parts of Asia.

Job Specialization As techniques for raising crops and domesticating and breeding animals improved, societies began to produce more food than they needed. Societies also became larger and more permanently rooted to one location. For the first time in human history, not everyone was engaged in the gathering or production of food. As a result, job specialization emerged. While some people farmed or raised animals, others produced crafts, became involved in trade, or provided such goods as farming tools or clothing.

AGRICULTURAL SOCIETIES

The invention of the plow during the horticultural and pastoral societies is considered the **second social revolution**, and it led to the establishment of agricultural societies approximately five thousand to six thousand years ago. Members of an **agricultural** or **agrarian society** tend crops with an animal harnessed to a plow. The use of animals to pull a plow eventually led to the creation of cities and formed the basic structure of most modern societies.

The development of agricultural societies followed this general sequence:

- Animals are used to pull plows.
- Larger areas of land can then be cultivated.
- As the soil is aerated during plowing, it yields more crops for longer periods of time.
- Productivity increases, and as long as there is plenty of food, people do not have to move.

- Towns form, and then cities.

- As crop yields are high, it is no longer necessary for every member of the society to engage in some form of farming, so some people begin developing other skills. Job specialization increases.

- Fewer people are directly involved with the production of food, and the economy becomes more complex.

Around this same time, the wheel was invented, along with writing, numbers, and what we would today call the arts. However, the invention of the steam engine—**the third social revolution**—was what took humans from agricultural to industrial society.

Roots of Gender Inequality As people moved toward domesticating animals and using them to do work, males tended to dominate more of the workforce, since physical strength was necessary to control animals. By the time societies became agricultural, males all but dominated the production of food. Since then, more prestige has been accorded to traditionally male jobs than to traditionally female jobs, and hence, to males more than to females.

INDUSTRIAL SOCIETIES

An **industrial society** uses advanced sources of energy, rather than humans and animals, to run large machinery. Industrialization began in the mid-1700s, when the steam engine was first used in Great Britain as a means of running other machines. By the twentieth century, industrialized societies had changed dramatically:

- People and goods traversed much longer distances because of innovations in transportation, such as the train and the steamship.

- Rural areas lost population because more and more people were engaged in factory work and had to move to the cities.

- Fewer people were needed in agriculture, and societies became **urbanized**, which means that the majority of the population lived within commuting distance of a major city.

- Suburbs grew up around cities to provide city-dwellers with alternative places to live.

The twentieth century also saw the invention of the automobile and the harnessing of electricity, leading to faster and easier transportation, better food storage, mass communication, and much more. Occupational specialization became even more pronounced, and a person's vocation became more of an identifier than his or her family ties, as was common in nonindustrial societies.

Gemeinschaft and Gesellschaft Sociologist **Ferdinand Tönnies** *divided societies into two large categories:* Gemeinschaft *societies and* Gesellschaft *societies.* Gemeinschaft *societies consist primarily of villages in which everyone knows everyone else. Relationships are lifelong and based on kinship. A* Gesellschaft *society is modernized. People have little in common with one another, and relationships are short term and based on self-interest, with little concern for the well-being of others.*

POSTINDUSTRIAL SOCIETIES

The Industrial Revolution transformed Western societies in many unexpected ways. All the machines and inventions for producing and transporting goods reduced the need for human labor so much that the economy transformed again, from an industrial to a postindustrial economy.

A **postindustrial society**, the type of society that has developed over the past few decades, features an economy based on services and technology, not production. There are three major characteristics of a postindustrial economy:

1. **Focus on ideas:** Tangible goods no longer drive the economy.

2. **Need for higher education:** Factory work does not require advanced training, and the new focus on information and technology means that people must pursue greater education.

3. **Shift in workplace from cities to homes:** New communications technology allows work to be performed from a variety of locations.

MASS SOCIETY

As industrialized societies grow and develop, they become increasingly different from their less industrialized counterparts. As they become larger, they evolve into large, impersonal mass societies. In a **mass society**, individual achievement is valued over kinship ties, and people often feel isolated from one another. Personal incomes are generally high, and there is great diversity among people.

Norms

Every society has expectations about how its members should and should not behave. A **norm** is a guideline or an expectation for behavior. Each society makes up its own rules for behavior and decides when those rules have been violated and what to do about it. Norms change constantly.

HOW NORMS DIFFER

Norms differ widely among societies, and they can even differ from group to group within the same society.

- **Different settings:** Wherever we go, expectations are placed on our behavior. Even within the same society, these norms change from setting to setting.

    EXAMPLE: *The way we are expected to behave in church differs from the way we are expected to behave at a party, which also differs from the way we should behave in a classroom.*

- **Different countries:** Norms are place-specific, and what is considered appropriate in one country may be considered highly inappropriate in another.

> EXAMPLE: *In some African countries, it's acceptable for peo-*
> *ple in movie theaters to yell frequently and make loud com-*
> *ments about the film. In the United States, people are*
> *expected to sit quietly during a movie, and shouting would be*
> *unacceptable.*

- **Different time periods:** Appropriate and inappropriate behavior often changes dramatically from one generation to the next. Norms can and do shift over time.

> EXAMPLE: *In the United States in the 1950s, a woman*
> *almost never asked a man out on a date, nor did she pay for*
> *the date. While some traditional norms for dating prevail,*
> *most women today feel comfortable asking men out on dates*
> *and paying for some or even all of the expenses.*

NORM CATEGORIES

Sociologists have separated norms into four categories: folkways, mores, laws, and taboos.

Folkways

A **folkway** is a norm for everyday behavior that people follow for the sake of convenience or tradition. People practice folkways simply because they have done things that way for a long time. Violating a folkway does not usually have serious consequences.

> EXAMPLE: *Holding the door open for a person right behind*
> *you is a folkway.*

Mores

A **more** (pronounced MORE-ay) is a norm based on morality, or definitions of right and wrong. Since mores have moral signifi-cance, people feel strongly about them, and violating a more usu-ally results in disapproval.

> EXAMPLE: *Parents who believe in the more that only married people should live together will disapprove of their son living with his girlfriend. They may consider their son's action a violation of the moral guidelines for behavior.*

Laws

A **law** is a norm that is written down and enforced by an official agency. Violating a law results in a specific punishment.

> EXAMPLE: *It is illegal in most countries to drive a car while drunk, and a person violating this law may get cited for driving under the influence (DUI), which may bring a fine, loss of driver's license, or even jail time.*

Taboos

A **taboo** is a norm that society holds so strongly that violating it results in extreme disgust. The violator is often considered unfit to live in that society.

> EXAMPLE: *In most countries, cannibalism and incest are considered taboo. In some Muslim cultures, eating pork is taboo because the pig is considered unclean.*

DEVIANCE

Where there are rules, there are rule breakers. Sociologists call the violation of a norm **deviance**. The word *deviant* has taken on the negative connotation of someone who behaves in disgusting or immoral ways, but to sociologists, a **deviant** is anyone who doesn't follow a norm, in either a good way *or* a bad way. See Chapter 6 for more about deviance.

> EXAMPLE: *Most people don't graduate from college with a 4.0 grade point average, so sociologists view someone who does graduate with a 4.0 as deviant. Likewise, most Americans get married at some point in their lives, so someone who chooses not to marry is sociologically a deviant.*

Although deviance can be good and even admirable, few societies could tolerate the chaos that would result from every person doing whatever he or she pleased. **Social control** refers to the methods that societies devise to encourage people to observe norms. The most common method for maintaining social control is the use of **sanctions**, which are socially constructed expressions of approval or disapproval. Sanctions can be positive or negative, and the ways societies devise to positively or negatively sanction behaviors are limited only by the society's imagination.

Positive Sanctions

A **positive sanction** rewards someone for following a norm and serves to encourage the continuance of a certain type of behavior.

> *EXAMPLE: A person who performs well at his or her job and is given a salary raise or a promotion is receiving a positive sanction. When parents reward a child with money for earning good grades, they are positively sanctioning that child's behavior.*

Negative Sanctions

A **negative sanction** is a way of communicating that a society, or some group in that society, does not approve of a particular behavior. The optimal effect of a negative sanction is to discourage the continuation of a certain type of behavior.

> *EXAMPLE: Imprisoning a criminal for breaking the law, cutting off a thief's hands for stealing, and taking away a teenager's television privileges for breaking curfew are all negative sanctions.*

Positive or Negative? A sanction is not always clearly positive or negative. A child who throws a temper tantrum may find he has everyone's attention, but while his parents might be telling him to stop, the attention he receives for his behavior is actually a positive sanction. It increases the likelihood that he'll do it again. Attention can be a powerful positive sanction, while lack of attention can be a strong negative sanction.

Norms and Consequences

Norm	Example	Consequences for violation
Folkway	Wearing a suit to an interview	Raised eyebrow
More	Only married couples should live together	Conflicts with family members, disapproval
Law	Laws against public nudity	Imprisonment, monetary fine
Taboo	Eating human flesh	Visible signs of disgust, expulsion from society

Status and Roles

Most people associate status with the prestige of a person's lifestyle, education, or vocation. According to sociologists, **status** describes the position a person occupies in a particular setting. We all occupy several statuses and play the roles that may be associated with them. A **role** is the set of norms, values, behaviors, and personality characteristics attached to a status. An individual may occupy the statuses of student, employee, and club president and play one or more roles with each one.

EXAMPLE:

Status as student
Role 1: Classroom: Attending class, taking notes, and communicating with the professor
Role 2: Fellow student: Participating in study groups, sharing ideas, quizzing other students

Status as employee
Role 1: Warehouse: Unloading boxes, labeling products, restocking shelves
Role 2: Customer service: Answering questions, solving problems, researching information

Status as club president
Role 1: Administrative: Running club meetings, delegating tasks to club members
Role 2: Public: Distributing flyers, answering questions, planning community volunteer activities

At any given time, the individual described above can also occupy the statuses of athlete, date, confidant, or a number of others, depending on the setting. With each change of status, the individual plays a different role or roles.

Society's Definition of "Roles" *Societies decide what is considered appropriate role behavior for different statuses. For example, every society has the "mother" status. However, some societies consider it inappropriate for a mother to assume the role of authority in the family. Other societies ascribe lots of power to the status of mother. In some societies, students are expected to be completely obedient to teachers. In American society, the student role involves asking the teacher questions and even challenging the teacher's statements.*

ROLE CONFLICT

Role conflict results from the competing demands of two or more roles that vie for our time and energy. The more statuses we have, and the more roles we take on, the more likely we are to experience role conflict.

A member of a nonindustrialized society generally has just a few statuses, such as spouse, parent, and villager. A typical middle-class American woman, meanwhile, probably has many statuses, and therefore many roles. She may be a mother, wife, neighbor, member of the PTA, employee, boss, town council president, and part-time student. Because people in modernized societies have so many roles, they are more likely than people in nonindustrialized societies to experience role conflict.

EXAMPLE: A working father is expected at work on time but is late because one of his children is sick. His roles as father and employee are then in conflict. A role for his father status dictates that he care for his sick child, while a role for his employee status demands that he arrive at work on time.

Culture

Culture is everything made, learned, or shared by the members of a society, including values, beliefs, behaviors, and material objects.

Culture is learned, and it varies tremendously from society to society. We begin learning our culture from the moment we're born, as the people who raise us encourage certain behaviors and teach their version of right and wrong. Although cultures vary dramatically, they all consist of two parts: **material culture** and **nonmaterial culture**.

MATERIAL CULTURE

Material culture consists of the concrete, visible parts of a culture, such as food, clothing, cars, weapons, and buildings. Aspects of material culture differ from society to society. Here are a few features of modern material culture in the United States:

- Soy lattes
- CD burners
- Running shoes
- iPods
- Lifestyle magazines
- Organic vegetables
- Sport utility vehicles

EXAMPLE: One common form of material culture is jewelry that indicates a person's status as married. In American culture, people wear a metal band on the ring finger of the left hand to show that they are married. In smaller, nonindustrialized societies, everyone knows everyone else, so no such sign is needed. In certain parts of India, women wear a necklace to indicate that they are married. In Northern Europe, married people wear wedding bands on the right hand.

NONMATERIAL CULTURE

Nonmaterial culture consists of the intangible aspects of a culture, such as values and beliefs. Nonmaterial culture consists of concepts and ideas that shape who we are and make us different from members of other societies.

*   A **value** is a culturally approved concept about what is right or wrong, desirable or undesirable. Values are a culture's principles about how things should be and differ greatly from society to society.

    EXAMPLE: In the United States today, many women value thinness as a standard of beauty. In Ghana, however, most people would consider American fashion models sickly and undesirable. In that culture and others, robustness is valued over skinniness as a marker of beauty.

Cult of the Car *Automobile ownership clearly illustrates the American value of material acquisition. Americans love cars, and society is constructed to accommodate them. We have a system of interstate roadways, convenient gas stations, and many car dealerships. Businesses consider where patrons will park, and architects design homes with spaces for one or more cars. A society that values the environment more than the material acquisition might refuse to build roadways because of the damage they might do to the local wildlife.*

- **Beliefs** are specific ideas that people feel to be true. Values support beliefs.

    EXAMPLE: Americans believe in freedom of speech, and they believe they should be able to say whatever they want without fear of reprisal from the government. Many Americans value freedom as the right of all people and believe that people should be left to pursue their lives the way they want with minimal interference from the government.

Hierarchy of Cultures

In societies where there are different kinds of people, one group is usually larger or more powerful than the others. Generally, societies consist of a dominant culture, subcultures, and countercultures.

DOMINANT CULTURE

The **dominant culture** in a society is the group whose members are in the majority or who wield more power than other groups. In the United States, the dominant culture is that of white, middle-class, Protestant people of northern European descent. There are more white people here than African Americans, Latinos, Asian Americans, or Native Americans, and there are more middle-class people than there are rich or poor people.

The Majority Doesn't Always Rule A group does not have to be a majority to be a dominant culture. In South Africa, there are four times as many black Africans as white Africans of European descent. Yet under a system of racial segregation and domination called apartheid, which was legally in effect from 1948 to 1991, the white population managed to hold political and economic power. South African whites thus were the dominant culture.

SUBCULTURE

A **subculture** is a group that lives differently from, but not opposed to, the dominant culture. A subculture is a culture within a culture. For example, Jews form a subculture in the largely Christian United States. Catholics also form a subculture, since the majority of Americans are Protestant. Members of these subcultures do belong to the dominant culture but also have a material and nonmaterial culture specific to their subcultures.

Religion is not the only defining aspect of a subculture. The following elements can also define a subculture:

- Occupation
- Financial status
- Political ideals
- Sexual orientation
- Age
- Geographical location
- Hobbies

W. E. B. Du Bois

One important theorist of subcultures was **W. E. B. Du Bois**. The first African American to receive a Ph.D. from Harvard University, Du Bois was one of the most renowned sociologists of race relations in the United States. He described racism as the predominant problem that American culture faced in the twentieth century. He paid special attention to the effects of what he called the "color line" in America and studied the impact of racism on both whites and blacks.

COUNTERCULTURE

A **counterculture** is a subculture that opposes the dominant culture. For example, the hippies of the 1960s were a countercul-ture, as they opposed the core values held by most citizens of the United States. Hippies eschewed material possessions and the accumulation of wealth, rejected the traditional marriage norm, and espoused what they called *free love*, which was basically the freedom to have sex outside of marriage. Though hippies were generally peaceful, they opposed almost everything the dominant culture stood for.

Not all countercultures are nonviolent. In 1995, the federal building in Oklahoma City, Oklahoma, was blown up, killing 168 people and injuring many others. That horrific crime brought to light the existence of another counterculture in the United States: rural militias. While such groups go by several names, their members tend to be people who despise the U.S. government for what they see as its interference in the lives of citizens.

Counterculture and Politics In many parts of the world, ethnic, political, or religious groups within larger nations struggle for independence or dominance. For generations, the Basque separatist group ETA (Freedom for the Basque Homeland) in northern Spain has violently pursued the goal of independence for the Basque regions. In Northern Ireland, which is governed by Great Britian, Sinn Fein is a violent political organization whose stated goal is the end of British rule in Ireland. ETA and Sinn Fein are examples of countercultures.

CHAPTER 1

SOCIETY AND CULTURE

The Interaction of Cultures

When many different cultures live together in one society, misunderstandings, biases, and judgments are inevitable—but fair evaluations, relationships, and learning experiences are also possible. Cultures cannot remain entirely separate, no matter how different they are, and the resulting effects are varied and widespread.

ETHNOCENTRISM

Ethnocentrism is the tendency to judge another culture by the standards of one's own culture. Ethnocentrism usually entails the notion that one's own culture is superior to everyone else's.

> EXAMPLE: *Americans tend to value technological advancement, industrialization, and the accumulation of wealth. An American, applying his or her own standards to a culture that does not value those things, may view that culture as "primitive" or "uncivilized." Such labels are not just statements but judgments: they imply that it is better to be urbanized and industrialized than it is to carry on another kind of lifestyle.*
>
> *People in other cultures, such as some European cultures, also see American culture through the lens of their own ethnocentrism. To members of other cultures, Americans may seem materialistic, brash, or arrogant, with little intellectual subtlety or spirituality. Many Americans would disagree with that assessment.*

Exported Ethnocentrism *When missionaries go to other countries to convert the local people to their brand of religion, they are practicing ethnocentrism. Missionaries usually want to convert people to their own forms of worship, and they sometimes encourage people to give up their religious beliefs.*

CULTURAL RELATIVISM

The opposite of ethnocentrism is **cultural relativism**—the examination of a cultural trait within the context of that culture. Cultural relativists try to understand unfamiliar values and norms without judging them and without applying the standards of their own culture.

> EXAMPLE: *In India, the concepts of dating, love, and marriage differ from those in the United States. Though love is important, parents choose their children's spouses according to similarities in educational levels, religions, castes, and family backgrounds. The families trust that love will develop over time but believe that a wedding can take place without it. From an American ethnocentric perspective, arranging marriages appears to be a custom that limits individual freedom. On the other hand, a cultural relativist would acknowledge that arranged marriages serve an important function in India and other cultures.*

CULTURE SHOCK

The practices of other cultures can be and often are jarring, and even the most adept cultural relativist is not immune to culture shock. **Culture shock** is the surprise, disorientation, and fear people can experience when they encounter a new culture.

> EXAMPLE: *Visitors to Western Europe from Islamic countries often experience culture shock when they see women wearing what they consider to be revealing clothing and unmarried couples kissing or holding hands in public, because these behaviors are forbidden or frowned upon in their own cultures.*

Culture Shock at Home *Encountering an unfamiliar subculture in one's own country, spending time with very rich or very poor people, or spending time with a group of people who hold radical or unfamiliar political views can produce culture shock just as much as encountering a brand-new culture in a foreign country.*

CHAPTER 1

SOCIETY AND CULTURE

CULTURE LAG

In 1922, the sociologist **William Ogburn** coined the term *culture lag*. **Culture lag** refers to the tendency for changes in material and nonmaterial culture to occur at different rates. Ogburn proposed that, in general, changes in nonmaterial culture tend to lag behind changes in material culture, including technological advances.

Technology progresses at a rapid rate, but our feelings and beliefs about it, part of our nonmaterial culture, lag behind our knowledge of how to enact technological change.

> EXAMPLE: *Though the technology that allows people to meet online has existed for years, an understanding of what the proper conduct is in an online "dating" situation lags behind the knowledge of how to use the technology. No definite answers exist to many important questions: How long should people talk over the internet before meeting in person? What is the right interval of response time between emails? New technology has brought with it new questions and uncertainties.*

CULTURAL DIFFUSION

Cultural diffusion is the process whereby an aspect of culture spreads throughout a culture or from one culture to another.

> EXAMPLE: *In the United States in the early 1990s, only people who needed to be available in emergencies, such as doctors, carried cell phones. Today, every member of a family may have his or her own cell phone. In some developing nations, where standard telephone lines and other communications infrastructures are unreliable or nonexistent, cell phones have been welcomed enthusiastically, as they provide people with an effective communication tool.*

Global Diffusion Many aspects of American culture, such as McDonald's hamburgers and Coca-Cola, have been diffused to other countries, and food items from other countries have become diffused throughout the United States. Sushi, for example, is now available in grocery stores in many parts of the country, and pizza can be found almost everywhere in the United States.

Imagine that you have just moved from New York City to a farm in rural Alabama. Which cultural aspects in your life would change, and which would remain the same? Be sure to give specific examples of how the hierarchy of the culture, your material and nonmaterial culture, and folkways and mores have changed.

Having just moved from New York City to rural Alabama, I have joined a new subculture. I am still an American and part of the national culture, but life in Alabama definitely represents a change from the subculture of a big city. I initially thought the biggest change would be in my material culture, but I have found that the nonmaterial aspects of culture are the most different from what I am accustomed to. In fact, I have experienced a kind of culture shock.

When I moved to Alabama, the first differences I noticed were in the physical environment. I saw farms and outbuildings instead of skyscrapers. People were driving trucks and SUVs; almost none were taking public transportation. Even people's clothing choices were different. In New York, wearing black is definitely part of the subculture. In Alabama, people wear more colorful clothing. In New York, I could wander the streets of the city and get a wireless Internet connection almost anywhere. The state of Alabama has one of the lowest rates of Internet access. I can't find a single wireless access point.

The more I looked around, however, the more I found that some aspects of my material culture hadn't really changed. The process of cultural diffusion ensured that I would have ready access to many of my favorites. I could still buy my daily frappuccino from the local Starbucks. I could still shop at Old Navy and The Gap. I could watch the same television shows. Cell phones are just as popular in Alabama as they are in New York. Despite the obvious change in the physical landscape, I could still re-create many aspects of my New York material culture.

Student Essay

The cultural aspects I found most jarring were nonmaterial. In particular, the values of rural Alabama are decidedly different than New York's. New York is a multicultural, liberal state. Alabama is a less heterogeneous, conservative state. Traditional, family values are celebrated in Alabama. These values exist in New York but aren't as central to life there because there are so many people in New York with different cultural backgrounds. For example, my newspaper in Alabama publishes a regular religion section every Saturday. Columnists assume that the majority of their readers are Christians. The closest equivalent in the *New York Times* is the Sunday Styles section devoted to fashion and weddings.

The folkways in Alabama also took me by surprise. For example, people commonly use "Ma'am" and "Sir" when addressing others. In fact, the use of "Yes, ma'am" and "Yes, sir" is expected. I encountered more than a few raised eyebrows when I simply said "Yes." Another difference I found in Alabama was that couples living together without being married seemed to violate a more of the society. In some instances, living together seemed to be a taboo that threatened the culprits with expulsion from their families. One woman I met gave her family a friend's address and phone number to hide the fact that she was living with her boyfriend.

My move to Alabama has proved to be a fascinating sociological experiment. I have discovered that in the United States, where the material aspects of the culture are so easily replicated, the nonmaterial aspects of a subculture are what make it different.

Sample Test Questions

1. How did the domestication of plants and animals change society?

2. In the United States, fast-food chains are part of the material culture. What values do these fast-food chains reflect? What parts of our material culture reflect the opposite values?

3. Compare and contrast subculture and counterculture.

4. How would you describe the dominant culture of the United States? What are some its values and beliefs?

5. Identify and describe a taboo in your culture. Why is that practice taboo? Is it taboo in other cultures?

6. Society is
   A. a political entity
   B. the same as culture or nation
   C. limited by geographical boundaries
   D. organized interaction of people sharing land and culture

7. Culture includes
   A. only material things such as cars or jewelry
   B. our thoughts, our beliefs, and our possessions
   C. the land we share
   D. only nonmaterial things such as values or beliefs

8. Which of the following types of societies came first?
   A. industrial
   B. agricultural
   C. mass
   D. horticultural and pastoral

9. *Kissing a person on both cheeks when you first meet is a French*
    A.   more
    B.   taboo
    C.   folkway
    D.   law

10. *In a sociological sense, earning a 4.0 GPA makes you a deviant because*
    A.   you only could have gotten that GPA by cheating
    B.   that GPA is not the norm
    C.   it alienates you from your peer group
    D.   it improves your status

ANSWERS

1. The domestication of plants and animals by hunting and gathering societies led to the birth of horticultural and pastoral societies. Horticultural societies planted crops and were able to stay in one place until they had exhausted the soil. Pastoral societies relied on the domestication and breeding of animals for food, allowing people to live in areas where crops did not grow. Because these societies were able to produce more food than they needed, people were able to concentrate on tasks other than food gathering. Job specialization emerged.

2. The popularity of fast-food chains in the United States demonstrates that Americans value speed and convenience over quality. The popularity of fast food shows that Americans favor instant gratification over sacrifice, even if what they are sacrificing is their health. Americans also don't value spending time at the dinner table as a family. On the other hand, Thanksgiving, a national holiday, stresses family and home-cooked food. Gyms and fitness equipment, meanwhile, reflect an American concern with fitness and health.

3. A subculture is way of living that is different from, but not opposed to, the dominant culture. In a pluralistic society, such as the United States, there are many subcultures. Religion, occupation, political ideals, and sexual orientation can define a subculture. A counterculture is a subculture that opposes the dominant culture, rejecting its values. For example, in the 1960s and 1970s, hippies in the United States eschewed material possessions and the accumulation of wealth.

4. The dominant culture of the United States is that of white, middle-class, Protestants of northern European descent. The dominant culture consists of people who are the most powerful and/or the most numerous. In the case of the United States, men are still considered the dominant culture, even if they aren't numerically superior. Some of America's shared values are freedom, equality, hard work, persistence, success, separation of church and state, and belief in the American dream.

5. Having sex with a close relative is taboo in American culture. Sex with a close relative is viewed negatively because it can produce genetically defective offspring. In addition to being a taboo, incest between some family members is against the law. In isolated countries, or among European royalty, marriages between cousins is accepted, but most cultures frown on sex between closer relatives.

6. **D**

7. **B**

8. **D**

9. **C**

10. **B**

Summary

What Is a Society?

- A **society** is a group of people with shared territory, interaction, and culture. Some societies are made up of people who are united by friendship or common interests. Some societies are merely social groups, two or more people who interact and identify with one another.

- Every society must have **territory**, or an area to call its own.

- Members of a society must interact with one another on a regular basis.

- **Culture** is a defining element of a society.

- Some societies are **pluralistic societies** composed of many different kinds of people, some of whom belonged to other societies. The United States is a pluralistic society.

- In a pluralistic society, members retain some ethnic traditions and beliefs from their old society. In order to fit into their new society, however, members must give up some of these original traditions. This process is called **assimilation**.

- In a truly pluralistic society, no one group is officially considered more influential than another.

Types of Societies

- Societies have evolved over many millennia. The different types of societies include **hunting and gathering**, **horticultural**, **pastoral**, **agricultural** or **agrarian**, **industrial**, and **postindustrial**.

- In **hunting and gathering societies**, members survive by gathering plants and hunting for food.

- Members of **horticultural societies** use hand tools to raise crops.

- Members of **pastoral societies** rely on domestication and breeding of animals for food.

- Members of **agricultural** or **agrarian societies** raise crops by harnessing an animal to a plow.

- In **industrial societies**, members use machinery to replace human labor in the production of goods. As fewer people are needed for agriculture, societies become **urbanized**, which means that the majority of the population lives within commuting distance of a major city.

- **Postindustrial societies** feature an economy based on services and technology rather than production.

- A **mass society** is a large, impersonal society that values individual achievement over kinship ties.

Norms

- **Norms** are guidelines, standards of behavior that change depending on **context** and **location**. The four types of norms are **folkways**, **mores**, **laws**, and **taboos**.

- **Deviance** is the violation of a norm, whether for good or bad.

- Societies discourage deviance with **social controls**, such as **positive sanctions** (rewards for approved behavior) and **negative sanctions** (punishments for disapproved behavior).

Status and Roles

- We all occupy several **statuses,** or positions in particular settings, and play roles based on them.

- A **role** is a set of norms, values, and behaviors attached to a status.

- When we are expected to fulfill more than one role at the same time, we can experience **role conflict**.

Culture

- **Culture** is everything made, learned, or shared by the members of a society.

- Although cultures vary dramatically, they all are composed of **material culture** (physical things) and **nonmaterial culture** (intangible aspects such as **beliefs** and **values**).

- A **dominant culture** is the culture held by the majority or the most powerful. It usually maintains economic, political, and cultural power.

- A **subculture** is a culture within the dominant culture. The subculture does not oppose the dominant culture but does have its own material and nonmaterial cultures that the dominant culture does not share.

- A **counterculture** actively opposes the dominant culture.

- **Ethnocentrism** is the tendency to view other cultures by the standards of one's own culture. Ethnocentrists often consider their cultures superior to other cultures.

- The opposite of ethnocentrism, **cultural relativism**, means interpreting other cultures based on one's own standards.

- We experience **culture shock** when the practices of other cultures seem unfamiliar, scary, or shocking.

- **William Ogburn** coined the term **culture lag**, which occurs when material and nonmaterial culture develop at different rates. For example, culture lag sometimes leaves us with technology we're not yet sure how to use.

- **Cultural diffusion** occurs when an item of culture spreads throughout a culture or from one culture to another.

Socialization

- Primary Socialization
- Resocialization
- Anticipatory Socialization
- Gender Socialization

2

In 1970, François Truffaut directed a movie called *L'Enfant Sauvage* (*The Wild Child*). It was allegedly a true story about two Frenchmen in the latter part of the eighteenth century who were walking in the countryside and came across a boy who appeared to be somewhere between six and eight years old. He couldn't speak, walk, or relate to humans. It seemed he had raised himself, perhaps with the help of certain animals. The two men took the boy to Paris, where a doctor worked with him intensively for many years. Eventually, the boy was able to function in French society.

Unlike some species of animals, and unlike what we sometimes see in movies, we cannot raise ourselves—we must be raised by other people, who teach us language, manners, beliefs, and much more. What we learn from the people who raise us is called our *socialization*, and it's a learning process that helps prepare us for a place in adult life. Socialization doesn't end with the advent of adulthood. As we grow and mature, we become members of new groups and must learn new things in order to function in our new roles.

Primary Socialization

Socialization is the process whereby we learn to become competent members of a group. **Primary socialization** is the learning we experience from the people who raise us. In order for children to grow and thrive, caregivers must satisfy their physical needs, including food, clothing, and shelter. Caregivers must also teach children what they need to know in order to function as members of a society, including norms, values, and language. If children do not receive adequate primary socialization, they tend not to fare well as adults.

DEVELOPMENTAL STAGES

Researchers have different theories about how children learn about themselves and their roles in society. Some of these theories contradict each other, and each is criticized for different reasons, but each still plays an important role in sociological thought.

Freud's Theory of Personality Development

Austrian physician **Sigmund Freud**, the founder of psychoanalysis, believed that basic biological instincts combine with societal factors to shape personalities. Freud posited that the mind consists of three parts that must interact properly for a person to function well in society. If any one of the three parts becomes dominant, personal and social problems may result. The three parts are the id, the superego, and the ego.

1. **Id:** According to Freud, the id develops first. A newborn's mind consists only of the id, which is responsible for the satisfaction of physical desires. The id represents a human being's most primitive desires, and a person ruled only by the id would do everything strictly for his or her own pleasure, breaking societal norms in the process and risking punishment.

2. **Superego:** As children move from infancy into childhood, their minds develop a superego, or conscience, which encourages conformity to societal norms and values. Someone with a hyperactive superego would be confined within a too-rigid system of rules, which would inhibit his or her ability to live normally.

3. **Ego:** A healthy mind also consists of the ego, or the part of the mind that resolves the conflicts between the id and the superego. Normally, the ego balances the desires of the id and superego, but when it fails, a person may have difficulty making decisions, which can lead to behavioral problems.

Mead's Theory of Social Behaviorism

Sociologist **George Herbert Mead** believed that people develop self-images through interactions with other people. He argued that the **self**, which is the part of a person's personality consisting of self-awareness and self-image, is a product of social experience. He outlined four ideas about how the self develops:

1. **The self develops solely through social experience.** Mead rejected Freud's notion that personality is determined partly by biological drives.

2. **Social experience consists of the exchange of symbols.** Mead emphasized the particularly human use of language and other symbols to convey meaning.

3. **Knowing others' intentions requires imagining the situation from their perspectives.** Mead believed that social experience depends on our seeing ourselves as others do, or, as he coined it, "taking the role of the other."

4. **Understanding the role of the other results in self-awareness.** Mead posited that there is an active "I" self and an objective "me" self. The "I" self is active and initiates action. The "me" self continues, interrupts, or changes action depending on how others respond.

Mead believed that the key to self-development is understanding the role of the other. He also outlined steps in the process of development from birth to adulthood:

Mead's Model of the Development of the Social Self

STEP 1 Infants take the role of the other through imitation, mimicking behavior without understanding intentions.	**STEP 2** Children engage in play, taking the role of significant others, such as parents, and imag-ining things from the others' points of view.
STEP 3 Older children (by age seven) engage in more complex play and games involving many others at once.	**STEP 4** In the final stage, adults recognize the **generalized other,** or cultural norms and values one refers to in order to evaluate oneself.

Cooley's Theory of the Looking-Glass Self

Like Mead, sociologist **Charles Horton Cooley** believed that we form our self-images through interaction with other people. He was particularly interested in how significant others shape us as individuals. A **significant other** is someone whose opinions matter to us and who is in a position to influence our thinking, especially about ourselves. A significant other can be anyone, such as a parent, sibling, spouse, or best friend.

Cooley's theory of socialization involves his notion of the looking-glass self. The **looking-glass self** refers to a self-image that is based on how we think others see us. He posited a three-step process in developing this self:

STEP 1 We imagine that a significant other perceives us in a certain way.

STEP 2 We imagine that he or she makes a judgment about us based on that perception.

STEP 3 We form a self-image based on how we think our significant other sees us.

Take This Term and Run with It In American society, we use the term significant other *to mean a romantic partner, but sociologists use the term differently (see page 44), and their usage was the original usage. The term* significant other *is just one example of a sociological term that has been appropriated by the public.*

Piaget's Theory of Cognitive Development

Swiss psychologist **Jean Piaget** began to investigate how children think when he was giving them intelligence tests. According to Piaget, the way children think changes as they mature physically and interact with the world around them. Piaget identified four periods of development: sensorimotor, preoperational, concrete operational, and formal operational.

STAGE 1: SENSORIMOTOR PERIOD (birth to roughly age two): During this stage, children learn by using their senses and moving around. The main achievement of this stage is **object permanence**, which is the ability to recognize that an object can exist even when it's no longer perceived or in one's sight.

> *EXAMPLE If a three-month-old baby sees a ball, she'll probably be fascinated by it. But if someone hides the ball, the baby won't show any interest in looking for it. For a very young child, out of sight is literally out of mind. When the baby is older and has acquired object permanence, she will start to look for things that are hidden because she will know that things can exist even when they can't be seen.*

STAGE 2: PREOPERATIONAL PERIOD (age two to seven): During this period, children keep getting better at symbolic thought, but they can't yet reason. According to Piaget, children aren't capable of conservation during this stage. **Conservation** is the ability to recognize that measurable physical features of objects, such as length, area, and volume, can be the same even when objects appear different.

EXAMPLE: Suppose a researcher gives a three-year-old girl two full bottles of juice. The girl will agree that they both contain the same amount of juice. But if the researcher pours the contents of one bottle into a short, fat tumbler, the girl will then say that the bottle has more. She doesn't realize that the same volume of juice is conserved in the tumbler.

STAGE 3: CONCRETE OPERATIONAL PERIOD (age seven to eleven): During this period, children start to become capable of performing mental operations or working problems and ideas through in their minds. However, they can perform operations only on tangible objects and real events.

EXAMPLE: If a mother tells her four-year-old, "Your Aunt Margaret is my sister," he may say, "No, she's not a sister, she's an aunt!" An eight-year-old is capable of grasping that Margaret can be both sister and aunt, as well as a daughter, wife, and mother.

STAGE 4: FORMAL OPERATIONAL PERIOD (age eleven through adulthood): During this period, children become capable of applying mental operations to abstract concepts. They can imagine and reason about hypothetical situations. From this point on, they start to think in abstract, systematic, and logical ways.

EXAMPLE: A teenager is motivated to organize a donation drive at his school for flood victims in Bangladesh because he is capable of imagining the plight of the Bangladeshis and empathizing with them. He is also capable of setting up the structures necessary to solicit and collect donations.

Piaget's Theory of Cognitive Development

Stage	Age
1. Sensorimotor	birth–2 years
2. Preoperational	2–7 years
3. Concrete Operational	7–11 years
4. Formal Operational	11 through adulthood

Kohlberg's Theory of Moral Development

Lawrence Kohlberg was interested in **moral reasoning,** or why people think the way they do about what's right and wrong. Influenced by Piaget, who believed that the way people think about morality depends on where they are in terms of cognitive development, Kohlberg proposed that people pass through three levels of moral development:

1. **The preconventional level:** Children ascribe great importance to the authority of adults.

2. **The conventional level:** Children want to follow rules in order to get approval.

3. **The postconventional level:** People are more flexible and think in terms of what's personally important to them. Only a small proportion of people reach this last stage of moral reasoning.

Psychologist **Carol Gilligan** argues that Kohlberg's theory was inaccurate because he studied only boys. Gilligan posits that girls look beyond the rules of morality to find the caring thing to do, even if that action breaks a preexisting rule. Girls and women are also less likely to judge an individual's actions as wrong because they see the complexities in relationships better than men do.

Criticisms of Development Theories Each of the theories of development has flaws. Freud's theories have always been controversial and are criticized today because they seem very male-centered. Piaget's theory of cognitive development is useful, but not all people reach the formal operational stage. Likewise, not all people reach Kohlberg's postconventional level of moral reasoning.

AGENTS OF SOCIALIZATION

People, groups, and experiences that influence our behavior and self-image are **agents of socialization.** Common agents of socialization for children include family, school, peer groups, and the mass media.

Family

The family is the agent of socialization with the most impact. From infancy through the teen years, most children rely almost solely on their parents or primary caregivers for basic necessities, nurturing, and guidance. The family determines a child's race, language, religion, class, and political affiliation, all of which contribute heavily to the child's self-concept.

School

Schools introduce children to new knowledge, order, bureaucracy, and students from family backgrounds different from their own. The school experience also often pressures children to conform to gender roles.

Peer Groups

A **peer group** is a social group in which members are usually the same age and have interests and social position in common. By becoming part of a peer group, children begin to break away from their parents' authority and learn to make friends and decisions on their own. Peer groups have a large impact on a child's socialization. Pressure from peers to engage in behavior forbidden by parents, such as skipping school or drinking alcohol, can be difficult to resist.

Mass Media

The **mass media** are methods of communication that direct messages and entertainment at a wide audience. Newspapers, magazines, television, radio, the internet, and movies are all forms of mass media. Numerous sociological studies attest to the profound influence of mass media on children. Racial and sexual stereotypes, violent and sexually explicit images, and unrealistic or even unhealthy beauty standards that appear in the mass media shape the way children think about themselves and their world.

Conflicting Agents of Socialization Different agents of socialization often teach children conflicting lessons. For example, in the family, children usually learn to respect their elders. Among their friends, however, children may learn that respecting adults makes them unpopular.

ISOLATED CHILDREN

Children raised in isolation, cut off from all but the most necessary human contact, do not acquire basic social skills, such as language and the ability to interact with other humans. Two of the most famous cases are Anna and Isabelle, both of whom were isolated from other human beings but had enough of their physical needs met to survive.

The Case of Anna

Anna was born in Pennsylvania to an unwed mother. The mother's father was so enraged at Anna's illegitimacy that the mother kept Anna in a storage room and fed her barely enough to stay alive. She never left the storage room or had anything but minimal contact with another human for five years. When authorities found her in 1938, she was physically wasted and unable to smile or speak. After intensive therapy, Anna did make some progress. She eventually learned to use some words and feed herself.

The Case of Isabelle

Isabelle was discovered in Ohio in the 1930s at the age of six. She had lived her entire life in a dark attic with her deaf-mute mother, after her grandfather decided he couldn't bear the embarrassment of having a daughter with an illegitimate child. He had banished both of them to the attic, where they lived in darkness and isolation. When Isabelle was discovered, she couldn't speak. After about two years of intensive work with language specialists, Isabelle acquired a vocabulary of about 2,000 words and went on to have a relatively normal life.

Isolated Monkeys In the 1960s, psychologists **Henry and Margaret Harlow** subjected rhesus monkeys to various conditions of social isolation. The behavior of rhesus monkeys is strikingly similar to the behavior of human beings in many ways. The Harlows found that monkeys placed in complete isolation for more than six months were unable to function normally once returned to the group. These monkeys were nervous and anxious. Their findings mirrored findings about isolated children such as Anna.

INSTITUTIONALIZED CHILDREN

Children raised in institutions such as orphanages often have difficulty establishing and maintaining close bonds with other people. Such children often have their physical needs met, but little else. They are fed, diapered, and kept warm but are deprived of significant contact with nurturing adults. They are not played with, cuddled, or spoken to. Such children tend to score lower on intelligence tests than children who were not only raised but also nurtured, and their interactions with other people reflect the fact that their emotional needs were not met.

Resocialization

The primary socialization received in childhood is just one part of the lifelong socialization process. Adults go through a process of **resocialization,** which is the learning of new norms and values that occurs when they join a new group or when life circumstances change dramatically. Learning new norms and values enables people to adapt, though newly learned things may contradict what was previously learned.

Though senility and certain diseases associated with old age can impair a person's ability to learn and adapt to new situations, many adults experience change throughout life. A new job, the loss of friends or a spouse, children leaving home, and retirement are all milestones that require resocialization.

Most instances of resocialization are mild modifications, such as adapting to a new work environment. Extreme forms of the process can include joining the military, going to prison, or otherwise separating from mainstream society.

The Social Construction of Life Stages *Sociologists generally divide a person's life into five stages: childhood, adolescence, adulthood, old age, and dying. These stages are socially constructed, which means that different societies apply different definitions and assumptions to each stage. For example, in the United States, childhood is a relatively carefree time during which young people expect to have time to play and to receive care from adults. In other societies, income generated by the work children do is very important to the family, and childhood, like other life stages, is a time of work and struggle.*

THE WORKPLACE

The workplace is an agent of socialization—in this case, resocialization. A new job brings with it new norms and values, including the following:

- What papers to fill out
- What equipment to use
- What tasks to complete and when to complete them
- When to arrive at work
- When to take a break
- When to leave

The employing organization also has its own values. The socialization process involves learning how strictly the company enforces work-related norms, such as whether it's acceptable for people of different job levels to fraternize outside of working hours, or whether a very late arrival will incur some kind of punishment. During resocialization, people learn how to modify behavior to fit the new situation.

TOTAL INSTITUTIONS

Most Americans are socialized to think for themselves and make their own decisions about daily tasks. That changes when they are resocialized by what sociologist **Erving Goffman** labeled a total institution. A **total institution** is an organization or setting that has the following characteristics:

- Residents are not free to leave.

- All actions are determined and monitored by authority figures.

- Contact with outsiders is carefully controlled.

- The environment is highly standardized.

- Rules dictate when, where, and how members do things.

- Individuality is discouraged.

Examples of total institutions include prisons, mental hospitals, and the military. In these total institutions, part of the resocialization process includes the loss of some decision-making freedom. The military decides what its soldiers wear, how they spend their time, and when and what they eat. To be promoted to a higher rank, they must demonstrate that they have been resocialized and have successfully adapted to the military's norms and values.

> **The Drama of Life** Goffman also developed the concept of **dramaturgy**, the idea that life is like a never-ending play in which people are actors. Goffman believed that when we are born, we are thrust onto a stage called everyday life, and that our socialization consists of learning how to play our assigned roles from other people. We enact our roles in the company of others, who are in turn enacting their roles in interaction with us. He believed that whatever we do, we are playing out a role on the stage of life.

Anticipatory Socialization

Anticipatory socialization occurs when we start learning new norms and values in anticipation of a role we'll occupy in the future. Making necessary adjustments in advance makes the actual transition into the new role easier. Also, by adopting some of the norms and values of a future role, we can evaluate whether that role will be right for us when the time comes to assume it.

> *EXAMPLE: A police officer who is about to begin working the night shift adjusts his sleeping habits several weeks before his start date. He goes to bed an hour later each evening, anticipating his new schedule of staying awake all night and sleeping during the day. Likewise, some couples live together before getting married to see whether they feel comfortable in that future role. They test the role of spouse before committing to it legally.*

Gender Socialization

Society expects different attitudes and behaviors from boys and girls. **Gender socialization** is the tendency for boys and girls to be socialized differently. Boys are raised to conform to the male gender role, and girls are raised to conform to the female gender or role. A **gender role** is a set of behaviors, attitudes, and personality characteristics expected and encouraged of a person based on his or her sex.

INFLUENCE OF BIOLOGY

Experts disagree on whether differences between males and females result from innate, biological differences or from differences in the ways that boys and girls are socialized. In other words, experts disagree on whether differences between men and women are due to nature, nurture, or some combination of both.

EXAMPLE: There are some significant differences between female and male brains. The language center in the male brain is usually in the dominant (usually left) hemisphere, whereas females use both hemispheres of the brain to process language. This may explain why females seem to have stronger communication skills and relish interpersonal communication more than males and why, on average, girls learn to speak and read earlier than boys.

INFLUENCE OF FAMILY

Every culture has different guidelines about what is appropriate for males and females, and family members may socialize babies in gendered ways without consciously following that path. For example, in American society, the color pink is associated with girls and the color blue with boys. Even as tiny babies, boys and girls are dressed differently, according to what is considered "appropriate" for their respective sexes. Even parents who strive to achieve a less "gendered" parenting style unconsciously reinforce gender roles.

EXAMPLE: The toys and games parents select for children are often unconsciously intended to socialize them into the appropriate gender roles. Girls receive dolls in an attempt to socialize them into future roles as mothers. Since women are expected to be more nurturing than men, giving a girl a doll teaches her to care for it and fosters the value of caring for others. When boys receive dolls, they are likely to be action figures designed to bring out the alleged aggressive tendencies in boys.

INFLUENCE IN EDUCATION

As children enter the educational system, traditional expectations for boys and girls continue. In the past, much research focused on how teachers were shortchanging girls in the classroom. Teachers would focus on boys, calling on them more and challenging them. Because boys were believed to be more analytical, teachers assumed they would excel in math and science. Teachers encouraged them to go into careers that require a lot of math and science, such as computer science or engineering.

Research from the late 1990s, however, indicates that the current educational climate is failing boys. Boys are falling behind girls in school. The dropout rate for boys is rising. More boys are being diagnosed as learning disabled. The number of boys applying to college has declined. Some sociologists argue that current teaching methods favor girls' learning styles. Girls mature more quickly than boys and are able to focus and concentrate in class more easily.

> EXAMPLE: *Studies show that boys are more physically active than girls. This difference is greater when children are in elementary school. Boys may be less able to sit still during a lesson. They are often sent out of class as disruptive, which puts them behind in the schoolwork and can reinforce their problems in the classroom.*

What's So Funny About Male Nurses? Meet the Parents (2000), a movie starring Ben Stiller, got laughs nationwide for presenting a main character who was a male nurse. The fact that a male pursuing a career in nursing still seems laughable shows how ingrained some gender roles still are.

INFLUENCE ON CAREER CHOICE

If cultural expectations dictate that girls are more compassionate and nurturing than boys, then parents, teachers, and counselors will steer them toward fields that require patience and concern for other people, such as nursing, social work, or elementary school teaching. Though a girl who expresses a desire to become a nuclear engineer would probably no longer be explicitly discouraged, a boy with a similar goal would probably encounter more encouragement.

> EXAMPLE: *Women working in traditionally male occupations often hit a glass ceiling, an invisible barrier that keeps women from reaching executive positions. Men who work in traditionally female occupations, such as nursing, social work, or elementary school teaching, are often viewed as more qualified than women. These men often benefit from a glass escalator; they are paid more and promoted more quickly than their female counterparts.*

CHAPTER 2
SOCIALIZATION

What are the main agents of socialization for a college student in the United States?

Socialization is a lifelong learning process. At different stages of life, different agents of socialization assume importance. For a child, parents and/or primary caregivers are the agents of socialization with the most impact. As an adult, work and family may be equally important agents of socialization. As a college student, peer groups, the mass media, and school take on greater influence.

Perhaps the most influential agent of socialization in a college student's life is his or her peer group. College students often live communally—in dormitories, in fraternity or sorority houses, or in apartment complexes catering to college students. Students attend classes with other students; they spend their recreational time with other students. In short, college students spend a majority of their time around their peers. Removed from their families—often for the first time—college students are particularly susceptible to the influence of and pressure from their peers. Students quickly learn how to dress, talk, and act in order to fit in with their peer groups.

Mass media is also a very influential agent of socialization for college students. Television, the internet, movies, music, and video games provide images of how students should act or look. Newspapers and magazines are less influential agents of socialization for college students, because few college students read them regularly.

New technology has shaped how and when the mass media and peer groups can influence college students. Because of technology, students can be socialized at all hours of the day, no matter where they are. According to one national survey, over 90 percent of college students have cell phones. On their cell phones, students can receive text messages and advertising, watch movies, and play video games. Students also have access to email and instant messaging. All of these technological advances provide opportunities to teach students what society expects of them.

Student Essay

Technology has also changed the nature of the mass media. It can make the mass media, generally believed to be impersonal communication aimed at vast audiences, more personal. Even if a student does not see a particular movie, he or she can read reviews of it and discuss its merits on websites. Online chat rooms provide a sense of community for many students. These chat rooms or bulletin boards sometimes have strict rules of conduct and swift punishment for conduct violations. Someone who is banned from a chat room for inappropriate behavior is quickly socialized as to how to post properly.

For college students, education as an institution plays an important yet limited role in socialization. Unlike elementary school and high school, in which class size is limited and teachers know the names of their students, college classes can be so large that professors don't learn the names of any of their students. Professors and instructors are not necessarily significant agents of socialization. Rather, the college experience socializes students.

Much of college life is anticipatory socialization. Students spend their college years practicing being adults. College forces students to learn how to manage themselves, their time, and their responsibilities to a greater degree than when they were in high school. They learn about bureaucracy as they navigate degree requirements to graduate. The goal of higher education is to create responsible adults who can contribute to society.

Despite all the socialization that students receive in college, they will go through a process of resocialization after they graduate from college and start jobs in the "real world." Students will find new peer groups, be exposed to sources of media, and find that bosses and supervisors have replaced their professors and instructors. New graduates will learn that many norms of college life aren't acceptable in the working world.

Sample Test Questions

1. Compare and contrast primary socialization and resocialization.

2. What is Sigmund Freud's theory of personality development?

3. How do we acquire a self?

4. Following the overthrow in 1989 of Nicolae Ceausescu's oppressive regime in Romania, the world learned about thousands of children housed in decrepit orphanages. Westerners flocked to Romania to adopt these orphans. What kinds of socialization problems did some orphans experience after their adoption?

5. What is gender socialization? How and why does it happen?

6. What is socialization?
    A. a learning process that begins at birth and ends at adolescence
    B. an instinctual response to events
    C. a theory of moral development
    D. a lifelong learning process that begins when you are born and ends when you die

7. Which of the following is NOT an agent of socialization?
    A. mother
    B. friends
    C. pets
    D. television

8. Mead's concept of the generalized other is similar to what other concept?
    A. the looking-glass self
    B. the superego
    C. the id
    D. the sensorimotor period

9. **What is Erving Goffman's theory of dramaturgy?**
    A.   Life is a battle among the id, ego, and superego
    B.   People with socialization issues are too dramatic
    C.   Life is a never-ending play in which people are actors
    D.   Gender roles are predetermined at birth

10. **Jean Piaget is known for his study of**
    A.   cognitive development
    B.   moral development
    C.   personality development
    D.   social behaviorism

ANSWERS

1. Primary socialization and resocialization are both processes by which we learn to become competent members of a group. Primary socialization occurs when we are children and refers to the learning that we receive from the people who raise us. Socialization continues throughout childhood and can be influenced by family, school, peer groups, and the mass media. Resocialization occurs later in life, when we must adapt to changes. We must learn new norms and values whenever we encounter a new group or when life circumstances change dramatically. Most resocialization occurs in the workplace.

2. Freud believed that basic biological instincts combine with societal factors to shape our personalities. The mind, according to Freud, consists of three parts that must interact properly for a person to function well in society. These three parts are the id, superego, and ego. The id represents a human being's most primitive desires. The superego, also called the conscience, is the part of the mind that internalizes society's values about right and wrong. The ego resolves conflicts between the id and the superego. If any one part becomes dominant, the person might encounter personal and social problems.

3. Sociologists disagree about how we acquire a self, the part of a person's personality consisting of self-awareness and self-image. According to George Herbert Mead, the key to development of the self is "taking the role of the other," or putting ourselves in someone else's shoes. The self develops solely through social experience and interaction. As the self develops, we internalize the expectations of more and more people. Mead referred to this group as the generalized other. Charles Horton Cooley believed that the self developed in relation to a smaller group of people—significant others. A significant other is someone whose opinions matter to us and who is in a position to influence our thinking, particularly about ourselves. Cooley's looking-glass self refers to a self-image based on how we think others see us. We form a self-image based on the reflection we see in the social mirror of our significant other.

4. Newly adopted children faced the problems common to institutionalized children. These orphans, who had suffered mental and physical deprivation, had difficulty establishing and maintaining emotional connections with their new family. Many new parents who had hoped for loving relationships with their new children found instead that these orphans were unable to bond with them. Some orphans also suffered cognitive impairment. They were more likely than children who had been nurtured early on to score poorly on intelligence tests.

5. Gender socialization refers to the fact that boys and girls are raised differently. Some behaviors and attitudes that are considered appropriate for one sex are considered inappropriate for the other. For example, boys are given chemistry sets; they are encouraged to become analytical and learn how to fix things. Girls are given dolls; they are believed to be more nurturing and patient than boys. Schools, the media, and society in general reinforce gender roles. These roles—female as nurturer, male as provider—may have important biological and historical purposes but are largely unnecessary in modern society.

6. **D**

7. **C**

8. **B**

9. **C**

10. **A**

Summary

Primary Socialization

- **Socialization** is the process whereby we learn to become competent members of a group. **Primary socialization** is the learning we experience from the people who raise us.

- Researchers have many theories about the developmental stages that children experience.

- **Freud** theorized that the development of the **id**, **ego**, and **superego** occurs over time and that the three must be in balance.

- **Mead** developed a theory which posited that "self" is a product of social experience.

- **Cooley** developed the notion of the **looking-glass self**.

- **Piaget** posited four stages of cognitive development: **sensorimotor**, **preoperational**, **concrete operational**, and **formal operational**.

- **Kohlberg** developed a theory of moral development with three levels: **preconventional**, **conventional**, and **postconventional**.

- **Agents of socialization** are people, groups, and experiences that influence behavior and self-image. They include family, school, peer groups, and the mass media.

- **Isolated** or **institutionalized** children may not experience primary socialization and can suffer many social and psychological defects as a result.

Resocialization

- Primary socialization occurs in childhood. **Resocialization**, the learning of new norms and values, occurs later in life, when life circumstances change or when people join a new group.

- The workplace is an agent of resocialization.

- **Total institutions** are environments in which people are isolated from mainstream society and expected to adhere to rigid rules. They demand resocialization. Some examples of total institutions are prisons, mental institutions, and the military.

Anticipatory Socialization

- When we learn new norms and values in anticipation of a future role, we are practicing **anticipatory socialization**.

- Practicing new norms in advance makes the transition easier and lets us know whether the role is right for us.

Gender Socialization

- **Gender socialization** is the tendency for boys and girls to be socialized differently. The impact of gender socialization can be seen in family, education, and career choice.

CHAPTER 2
SOCIALIZATION

Social Institutions

- Economy
- Government
- Family
- Religion
- Education
- Medicine

3

The word *institution* conjures many different images: a stark building surrounded by a high metal fence; a town hall; a church; the building that houses the college president's office. To sociologists, however, an institution isn't a building; an institution is what goes on *inside* the building. An **institution** is a set of norms surrounding the carrying out of a function necessary for the survival of a society.

People in every society must fulfill certain functions in order to survive. They must set up processes for rearing and educating children. They must develop a system for maintaining order and managing relations with other societies. They must agree on methods for producing and exchanging goods and services. Societies differ in how they carry out these functions, but they all must somehow accomplish the same tasks in order to survive as a social unit. Institutions may seem abstract, but they are part of a world that is very real.

Economy

The **economy** is the institution that provides for the production and distribution of goods and services, which people in every society need. Sometimes they can provide these things for themselves, and sometimes they rely on others to provide them. When people rely on others for goods or services, they must have something to exchange, such as currency (in industrialized societies) or other goods or services (in nonindustrialized societies). The customs surrounding exchange and distribution of good and services shape societies in fundamental ways.

> *Macrosociology vs. microsociology* Sociologists use two approaches when studying society. In **macrosociology**, sociologists analyze large-scale social forces, such as institutions. They identify and analyze the structure of societies. The second approach sociologists use is **microsociology**, the study of social interaction. These sociologists focus on face-to-face interaction, how people act around others. This method is focused more on individuals than groups.

ECONOMIC SYSTEMS

The two dominant economic systems in the world are capitalism and socialism. Most societies have varying blends of the two systems. Common hybrids of capitalism and socialism are welfare capitalism and state capitalism.

Capitalism

Capitalism is a system under which resources and means of production are privately owned, citizens are encouraged to seek profit for themselves, and success or failure of an enterprise is determined by free-market competition.

> EXAMPLE: *The United States is one of the most purely capitalistic societies in the world. Most U.S. businesses are privately owned, but the government does regulate business practices.*

Socialism

Socialism is a system under which resources and means of production are owned by the society as a whole, rights to private property are limited, the good of the whole society is stressed more than individual profit, and the government maintains control of the economy.

> EXAMPLE: *China is a socialist country. The government owns and controls almost all natural resources.*

Welfare capitalism

Welfare capitalism is a system that features a market-based economy coupled with an extensive social welfare system that includes free health care and education for all citizens.

> EXAMPLE: *Sweden allows private business ownership, but the government controls a significant part of the economy. High taxes support an extensive array of social welfare programs.*

State capitalism

State capitalism is a system under which resources and means of production are privately owned but closely monitored and regulated by the government.

> EXAMPLE: *South Korea's government works closely with the country's major companies to ensure their success in the global marketplace.*

Socialism vs. Capitalism No one economic system has succeeded in satisfying all the needs of its citizens. Several economic studies over the past few generations have shown that, in general, citizens in societies with capitalist economies enjoy a higher standard of living than those in socialist societies.

SOCIAL INSTITUTIONS

CHAPTER 3

MARX'S ECONOMIC THEORY

Philosopher and historian **Karl Marx** believed that the economy was the basic institution of society and that all other institutions, such as family and education, served to fuel the economy. As societies became more industrialized, he theorized, they also became more capitalistic. Marx disliked the fact that capitalism created a two-tiered system consisting of factory owners and factory workers, in which the groups were constantly in conflict with each other. Factory owners wanted to pay their workers as little as possible to maximize profits. Factory workers, on the other hand, wanted to make as much money as possible. The advantage was always with the owners, who could choose to fire workers who wanted too much and hire workers who would work for less.

Marx was a **conflict theorist**, believing that in any capitalist society there was always conflict between the owners of the means of production and the workers. He believed that the only way to resolve the conflict was for workers to unite, mount a revolution, and overthrow their oppressors. Marx believed that once the dust settled after the revolution, all societies would be **communist**, meaning that all the means of production would be owned by everyone and all profits would be shared equally by everyone. His ideas inspired the Russian Revolution of 1917.

ECONOMIC TRENDS

The ways the world and the U.S. economies work are changing rapidly. There are several important trends:

- **Globalization:** The expansion of economic activity across many borders characterizes the global economy. Poorer, developing nations now produce the raw materials for the world's multinational corporations. These multinational companies control most of the world's economy.

- **Demand for educated professionals:** The postindustrial economy is driven by trained professionals such as lawyers, communications professionals, doctors, and teachers.

- **Self-employment:** New, affordable communications technology has allowed more people to go into business for themselves.

- **Diversity in the workplace:** Once the bastion of white males, professional offices are heavily populated by women and minorities in today's society.

Government

A **government** is an institution entrusted with making and enforcing the rules of a society as well as with regulating relations with other societies. In order to be considered a government, a ruling body must be recognized as such by the people it purports to govern. A person or group that considers itself the leading body of a society has no power if the members of the society do not recognize the person or group as such.

TYPES OF GOVERNMENTS

Most of the world's governments fall into one of four categories: monarchy, democracy, authoritarianism, or totalitarianism.

Monarchy

Monarchy is a political system in which a representative from one family controls the government and power is passed on through that family from generation to generation. Most of the world's monarchies are **constitutional monarchies**, in which the reigning member of the royal family is the symbolic head of state but elected officials actually do the governing. Many European countries have constitutional monarchies.

> EXAMPLE: *Saudi Arabia is a monarchy. Until recently it was an **absolute monarchy**, meaning that the king had complete control of the country. The Saud royal family introduced a constitution in 1992.*

Democracy

Democracy is a political system in which citizens periodically choose officials to run their government.

> EXAMPLE: *El Salvador has a democratic form of government. Throughout most of the nineteenth century, El Salvador was beset by revolution and war, and from 1931 to 1979 it was ruled by military dictators. From 1980 to 1992, the country was torn apart by civil war. The country currently has a stable government and elected president.*

Authoritarianism

Authoritarianism is a political system that does not allow citizens to participate in government.

> EXAMPLE: *Zimbabwe is controlled by an authoritarian leader whose human rights violations and disastrous economic policies have brought on international condemnation. However, not all authoritarian governments are outcasts. China has an authoritarian government, but it is a member of the World Trade Organization and a major player in international politics.*

Authoritarian or Totalitarian? There is disagreement among theorists about the exact difference between authoritarianism and totalitarianism. Both tend to use brutal tactics to suppress perceived opposition. Totalitarian governments, however, extend their control into virtually all aspects of people's lives and feature a "cult of personality" around their leader.

Totalitarianism

Totalitarianism is a political system under which the government maintains tight control over nearly all aspects of citizens' lives.

> EXAMPLE: *Cambodia under the regime of Pol Pot and the Khmer Rouge from 1976 to 1978 was totalitarian. Under the banner of socialism, Pol Pot attempted a radical reformation of Cambodia. He forced the evacuation of the country's cities and relocated citizens to communal farms in the countryside, where they were to be "reeducated" to become part of an idealized communist agrarian society. Pol Pot's secret police tortured and murdered over a million "dissenters," especially those he viewed as urban intellectuals.*

U.S. POLITICS

In the early years of America's nationhood, individualism and individual rights were valued above all else. Citizens of the United States wanted as little governmental interference in their lives as possible and believed that people should be free to make of their lives whatever they could. Today, most people in the United States recognize the need for government control of such things as schools, roads, and national defense, but citizens disagree about where to draw the line when it comes to the size and scope of government's involvement.

The Welfare State

A **welfare state** is a type of government in which the state provides for and promotes the social and economic well-being of its citizens. The government provides some sort of social insurance, or benefits, for families or individuals in dire need. The welfare state also includes provisions for government funding of education, health services, and housing.

Since the Great Depression and the New Deal, the United States has greatly increased the welfare programs it offers to its citizens. The amount the United States spends on welfare, however, is still much smaller than the amount spent by other Western nations.

In 1996, Congress ended the federal public assistance that guaranteed some income to all poor Americans.

Party Politics

The United States has a two-party political system, in which the Democratic Party and the Republic Party are the dominant political forces.

- The **Democratic Party** believes that the government should play an active role in promoting the general welfare of the country and takes a liberal stand on social issues.

- The **Republican Party** believes that the government should take a limited role in providing social services and takes a conservative stand on social issues.

*Weber's Power Theory Sociologist **Max Weber** identified **power**—the ability to achieve ends even in the face of resistance—as the foundation of government. Getting people to comply with a government's rule also requires authority, which is power people believe is just. Weber labeled three kinds of authority: **traditional authority**, which rests on well-established cultural patterns; **rational-legal authority**, which rests on rules and laws; and **charismatic authority**, which depends on the personal magnetism of one person.*

GOVERNMENTS IN CONFLICT

Conflicts in governments generally take three forms:

1. **Revolution:** A violent overthrow of the government by its citizens. Often, a group of charismatic philosophers and intellectuals sparks the movement.

2. **War:** Armed conflict between nations or societies. Societies have always waged war over rights to land and resources or because of conflicting moral, political, or religious objectives. In the twentieth century, the nature of war changed dramatically with the development of nuclear weapons. Massive stockpiling of weapons of mass destruction has made the threat of global annihilation a strong deterrent to war among industrialized nations.

3. **Terrorism:** A politically motivated violent attack on civilians by an individual or group. Since few nations have the military strength to attack the United States directly, terrorism by extremist groups within and outside the country has become an increasingly potent threat.

Family

The institution of **family** has three important functions:

1. To provide for the rearing of children

2. To provide a sense of identity or belonging among its members

3. To transmit culture between generations

In Western societies, we tend to think of a family as consisting of a mother, father, and children living under one roof: a **nuclear family**. Before societies modernize, families usually consist of several generations and branches of **extended family** living in the same dwelling, or in the same village. As modernization occurs, young people tend to move away from the villages in which they were raised in search of jobs, leaving the older generations behind. They relocate to cities and meet people they probably never would have met had they stayed home. People in modernized, urbanized societies meet spouses on their own, rather than being introduced by family members, and marry and settle down in locations that are often far from their original communities.

MARRIAGE

Marriage, a foundation of family life, exists in all cultures, with some variations:

- **Endogamy:** Marriage between members of the same category, class, or group

- **Exogamy:** Marriage between members of different categories, classes, or groups

- **Monogamy:** Marriage between one man and one woman

- **Polygamy:** Marriage between one man and more than one woman

- **Polyandry:** Marriage between one woman and more than one man

In some cultures, after marriage, a couple lives in the wife's family's household—a practice called **matrilocality**. When couples live in the husband's family's household, the practice is called **patriolocality**. If they go out and get their own place to live, they practice **neolocality**.

Divorce and Remarriage Once taboo, divorce is now common in the United States. Many factors have contributed to the tenfold increase in the U.S. divorce rate over the past century. Women have become less economically dependent on men, which means they are now able to leave unhappy marriages and support themselves. Legal standards have also relaxed, making divorce easier to obtain. Because the divorce rate is so high, so is the rate of remarriage. U.S. society is still coming to terms with the ramifications of blended families, those composed of children and parents from both present and past marriages.

CHILD-REARING

Rearing children is a primary function of a family. Being in a family provides children with a sense of identity. They learn the norms and values of their societies, as well as the norms and values of the smaller groups to which they belong. By learning about their cultural heritages, children gain a sense of belonging to something larger than themselves. By teaching children about their heritage, families insure their culture will live on.

Despite the many demands of child-rearing, most adults describe raising children as an important and fulfilling duty. Nevertheless, the number of children in the households of industrialized countries has been dwindling for generations. Economic pressures have led the average U.S. family to have only one or two children. Because both parents must often work outside the home to support the family, parents and children spend less and less time together.

ALTERNATIVE FAMILIES

Not all families are centered on a married couple with children. To an increasing degree, U.S. households feature alternative types of families, such as the following:

- Single-parent household

- Cohabitating, unmarried couples

- Gay and lesbian couples

- Single adults

Religion

Religion is a social institution that answers questions and explains the seemingly inexplicable. Religion provides explanations for why things happen and demystifies the ideas of birth and death. Religions based on the belief in a single deity are **monotheistic**. Those that encompass many deities are **polytheistic**.

> **Uniting Traditions** *When families attend religious services or put up decorations in honor of a holiday, they are teaching their children about their religion and how to observe it. By engaging in these activities and traditions, children are united with others of the same religion around the world. In this way, families teach their own culture as well as the culture of the society at large.*

MAJOR WORLD RELIGIONS

Most of the world subscribes to one of the following religions:

- **Christianity:** The most widespread world religion, Christianity derived from Judaism. It is based on the belief that Jesus Christ was the son of God and the redeemer of mankind. There are many different Christian denominations.

- **Islam:** Followers of Islam are called Muslims. Muslims believe that the true word of God was revealed to the prophet Muhammad around 570 A.D. God in Islam is the same god as the Christian and Judaic deity.

- **Judaism:** Judaism is a monotheistic religion that predates Christianity, built on the belief that they are the "chosen people" of God.

- **Hinduism:** Hinduism is the oldest major world religion, dominant in India. Hindus do not worship a single person or deity but rather are guided by a set of ancient cultural beliefs. They believe in the principle of karma, which is the wisdom or health of one's eternal soul. Karma can be strengthened with good acts and harmed by bad acts. Hindus believe that karma plays a role in reincarnation, a cycle of continuous rebirth through which, ideally, the soul can achieve spiritual perfection. The state of a person's karma determines in what form he or she will be reborn.

- **Buddhism:** Buddhists, most of whom live in Japan, Thailand, Cambodia, and Burma, follow the teachings of Siddhartha Gautama, a spiritual teacher of the sixth century B.C.E. Buddhism, like Hinduism, does not feature any single all-powerful deity but teaches that by eschewing materialism, one can transcend the "illusion" of life and achieve enlightenment.

TYPES OF RELIGIOUS GROUPS

Sociologists group religious organizations into three categories: church, sect, and cult.

- A **church** is a religious group integrated with society.

  EXAMPLE: The Roman Catholic Church is well integrated in the society in Spain.

- A **sect** is a religious group that sets itself apart from society as a whole.

  EXAMPLE: The Amish of Pennsylvania are a classic sect. Though Christian, they choose to set themselves apart from the rest of society by their lifestyle, which eschews many aspects of modernity.

- A **cult** is a religious group that is outside standard cultural norms, typically centered around a charismatic leader.

  EXAMPLE: The People's Temple, a cult that emerged in the late 1970s, was led by a man named Jim Jones. Jones started his cult in San Francisco, then convinced several hundred followers to move with him to Jonestown, Guyana. He claimed to be a god and insisted on strict loyalty. In 1978, he and 913 of his followers committed mass suicide.

RELIGION IN THE UNITED STATES

In the United States, the degree to which people are religious is related to their social class, race, and ethnicity. The most affluent people in the United States tend to be Protestant, although Jews also enjoy a higher-than-average standard of living. Northern Europe, which is mostly Protestant, was the area of origin for most of the early settlers in America, so people of Northern European descent tend to come from the most established families and encounter the least amount of prejudice. People who emigrated from predominantly Roman Catholic countries in Southern and Eastern Europe and, later, Latin America encountered more prejudice and tend to be less affluent than the Protestants. However, there is wide variation among the groups.

African-American churches have blended the traditions of Christianity and the African faiths of the slaves brought to America. These churches have played a major role in promoting civil rights for blacks.

The Rise of Fundamentalism *Fundamentalism is a strict, literal adherence to religious doctrine accompanied by a rejection of intellectualism and worldliness. All religions can experience a rise in fundamentalism. Among Southern Baptists, for example, fundamentalism has been on the rise. The Taliban regime in Afghanistan adhered to fundamentalist Muslim doctrine.*

Education

Every society has to prepare its young people for a place in adult life and teach them societal values through a process called **education**.

FUNCTION OF EDUCATION

Education is an important agent of socialization and encourages social integration, especially in countries with diverse populations, such as the United States. Through their schools, students from a variety of cultural backgrounds come into contact with mainstream culture.

UNEQUAL EDUCATION

The vast majority of the children in the United States attend public schools, but these schools are far from equal. Public schools located in affluent, predominantly white, suburban areas tend to have more modern facilities and smaller class sizes than schools in urban, less affluent areas, which means that economic status often determines the quality of education a student receives. Children whose parents are wealthy enough to send them to private school enjoy an even greater advantage. Studies show that graduates of private schools are more likely to finish college and get high-salary jobs than are graduates of public schools.

Medicine

The institution of **medicine** is responsible for defining and treating physical and mental illnesses among members of a society. The goal of a society's medical establishment is to promote **health**, the total well-being of its people. The nature of both health and medicine in a given society are culturally determined.

Definitions of illness vary widely from society to society. Societies attach different values to conditions that people worldwide experience, and as such, they treat those conditions differently, or not at all. In addition, societies have vastly differing views on the nature and origin of both physical and mental illness.

PHYSICAL ILLNESS

The institution of medicine must not only define illness but also figure out how to cure it. The acceptance of a cure depends on how that society views the illness. In the West, illnesses are thought to originate primarily from physical sources, and doctors use biomedical or surgical cures to treat them. Other cultures consider illnesses punishment for certain deeds or curses that are put on individuals, so other methods of curing the condition, such as incantations or folk remedies, are more common.

MENTAL ILLNESS

The symptoms and origins of a mental illness can be as varied as those of a physical illness. In the West, hearing voices or hallucinating are generally viewed as symptoms of a mental illness, such as schizophrenia. In other societies, these symptoms might instead indicate a religious experience, and the afflicted individual may not be seen as mentally ill. Instead, he or she could be viewed as enlightened or special in a positive way.

SCIENTIFIC MEDICINE

What Americans consider "medical treatment" is actually a fairly new approach to health care. Before the nineteenth century, any number of people might be called upon to treat a sick person: herbalists, druggists, midwives, even barbers (in the middle ages, barbers became skilled at bloodletting). Today, most Americans seek medical treatment from trained, certified medical doctors who focus on treating their particular illnesses and symptoms. This modern, scientific medical practice has been remarkably effective at saving people's lives. Women and children in particular have benefited, and rates of maternal death in childbirth and infant mortality have plummeted since the turn of the twentieth century.

Still, the scientific approach has its drawbacks. Practitioners tend to focus on only one part of the patient at a time and don't try to see the "big picture" of patient health or ask questions about the patient's diet, exercise habits, or emotional well-being, all of which might influence treatment.

HOLISTIC MEDICINE

Once scientific medicine became dominant in industrialized countries, practitioners of traditional forms of medicine, such as midwives, acupuncturists, and herbalists, were pushed to the fringe of the medical establishment, their work dismissed as quackery. But a growing body of evidence suggests that **holistic medicine**, a medical approach that involves learning about a patient's physical environment and mental status, may be just as effective as scientific medicine for some illnesses. More and more medical doctors are opening themselves to the possibility of a balance between holistic and scientific medicine.

During the 2004 U.S. presidential election, the issue of gay marriage divided the nation. How did this issue reflect the changing nature of the family institution? How have alternative families transformed the institution?

During the 2004 presidential election, opponents of gay marriage argued that it threatens the institution of marriage and thereby the family. These conservatives defined *marriage* as a relationship between a man and a woman; they defined *family* as a unit including a husband, a wife, and their children living together under one roof. Sociologists have known for years, however, that this stereotypical ideal does not reflect the reality of marriage and the family in the United States. To an increasing degree, American households feature alternative types of families. Single-parent households, people living alone, and unmarried couples have transformed the definition of family.

The nuclear family reached its peak in the 1950s. According to 2000 census data, only about one quarter of American families today are comprised of that structure. An equal number of families are single-parent households, due mainly to the high rate of divorce. Today, almost 50 percent of first marriages and 40 percent of second marriages end in divorce. Divorce rates have increased for a variety of reasons, primarily rising affluence and changing gender roles, both of which have transformed the needs of people in a modern marriage. Women no longer need to be married or to stay married for financial reasons, and both men and women have higher expectations for a happy marriage and are less likely to remain in an unhappy one.

These high expectations, as well as the fact that many Americans are delaying marriage, also contribute to the increasing number of adult Americans who live alone. The average age for first marriage for men and women is almost twenty-seven and twenty-five years old, respectively. People who are divorced or widowed often do not remarry. Some widows who might want to remarry find it increasingly difficult to find a mate, since as the American population ages, women outnumber men.

Student Essay

The rise in unmarried couples—both heterosexual and homosexual, with and without children—has probably played the greatest role in transforming the family. The number of cohabitating, unmarried couples has risen some 70 percent over the last decade. Their total number is still less than 5 percent, but their rapid growth signals an important shift in the institution. Americans are defining their own families, outside the prescribed norms, and society is responding. Whereas most businesses used to limit health and other benefits to legally recognized spouses of their employees, many have extended these benefits to domestic partners. Some states offer domestic partner registries, which confer some of the legal rights and protections of married couples to homosexual and heterosexual couples. Vermont is currently the only state offering a civil union, which confers on homosexual couples the same rights as married, heterosexual couples. Other states, however, do not have to honor that union, as they would have to honor the rights of a married couple.

People opposing gay marriage as a threat to the nuclear family have failed to realize that the family structure in the United States has already changed. Figuring out how these changes have affected and will affect American society will keep sociologists busy for years to come.

Sample Test Questions

1. Institutions fulfill functions necessary for the society to survive. In today's technologically oriented society, what would happen if there were no educational institutions? What would be the results for people seeking jobs, for the economy, and for families?

2. The U.S. government was founded on a belief in the separation of church and state. Yet when a new president takes the oath of office, he places his hand on a Bible. Do you believe we have achieved separation of church and state in the United States?

3. Compare and contrast capitalism and socialism. Which economic system do you believe provides a better foundation for a society?

4. How are the functions of education and the family similar? Can one take the place of the other? Why or why not?

5. Do you think a Hindu would practice holistic medicine or scientific medicine? What about a Christian?

6. A set of norms surrounding a necessary function of society is referred to as a(n)
   A. marriage
   B. institution
   C. authoritarianism
   D. government

7. You are a Brahmin (highest class) in India. You decide to marry an untouchable (lowest class). Sociologists would call this marriage an example of
   A. exogamy
   B. endogamy
   C. polygamy
   D. polyandry

8. *What was Karl Marx's contribution to the understanding of social institutions?*
    A.   As societies became more industrialized, they become more communist.
    B.   In a socialist society, the bosses and the workers are constantly in conflict with one another.
    C.   The economy is the basic institution in society.
    D.   None of the above

9. *What is the primary difference between a sect and a cult?*
    A.   A sect can be Christian or Jewish but not Islamic. All religions have cults.
    B.   Sects are monotheistic; cults are polytheistic.
    C.   A sect isn't really in conflict with social norms. A cult is outside social norms enough to seem extreme or even dangerous.
    D.   Sects have male authority figures; the leaders in cults can be either men or women.

10. *Which of the following is NOT a requirement of the government?*
    A.   To make and enforce the rules of society
    B.   To regulate relations with other societies
    C.   To have a leader whose power is recognized by the people
    D.   To promote the health of the public

ANSWERS

1. The absence of educational institutions would produce extreme social stratification. Only rich people would be able to afford to train their children for high-paying jobs. Poor people would have to train their children to start working in low-paying jobs as soon as possible. This situation could put enormous strains on the economy. There are fewer rich people than poor people, which means that there would be fewer children available to fill jobs requiring extensive training. Without qualified leadership, the economy would suffer. In addition, segregation would increase without the social interaction and integration provided by schools. Different social groups would have little way of interacting and learning about each other. Families would be more overburdened. Parents would have to find something else to do with their children all day. The children might be put to work or left unsupervised in potentially dangerous situations.

2. The U.S. government has succeeded in keeping church and state separate even if keeping the two separate remains a constant struggle. Many governmental decisions must be based on ideas of right and wrong. People's ideas of right and wrong generally come from religion. Since Christianity is the dominant U.S. religion, Christian beliefs often seep, or threaten to seep, into governmental policy.

3. Capitalism and socialism are the dominant economic systems in the world, but they have little else in common. Capitalism is a system under which the resources and means of production are privately owned. Citizens are encouraged to seek profit for themselves, and success or failure of an enterprise is determined by free-market competition. Under socialism, the society as a whole owns the resources and means of production. Rights to private property are limited. The good of the whole society is stressed more than individual profit, and the government maintains control of the economy. In general, the nations operating under capitalist systems have a higher standard of living than those with socialist economic systems. While capitalism does not offer support to all its citizens, it does offer greater opportunity for success than socialism. For that reason, capitalism provides a better foundation for a society.

4. Family and education are both important agents of socialization for children. These two institutions teach children what they need to know in order to function in a society as adults. They both transmit knowledge of society's values and culture. The two institutions are not interchangeable, however. From a practical standpoint, schools are not equipped to rear children, to provide for them 24 hours a day, as a family does. A family can provide a sense of identity or belonging to its members, but it does not offer children a chance to encounter different cultural or ethnic groups. Education encourages social integration, especially in countries with diverse populations, such as the United States. Through their schools, students from a variety of cultural backgrounds come into contact with mainstream culture.

5. A Hindu would most likely practice holistic medicine. The belief that a patient's physical environment and mental status are equally important seems similar to a Hindu's belief in karma. A Hindu may be sick because of bad karma, rather than a diagnosable illness. A holistic medical practitioner would be more likely to look at the big picture and ask questions about a person's emotional well-being. A Christian, particularly in the United States, would be more likely to turn to medical doctors. Christians' belief in a single, omnipotent power may reinforce their comfort with authority figures like doctors.

6. **B**

7. **A**

8. **C**

9. **C**

10. **D**

Summary

Economy

- The **economy** is the social institution responsible for the production and distribution of goods.

- The two dominant economic systems in the world are **capitalism**, under which resources and means of production are privately owned, and **socialism**, a system under which those resources are owned by the society as a whole.

- Welfare capitalism and state capitalism are hybrids of capitalism and socialism. **Welfare capitalism** features a market-based economy coupled with an extensive social welfare system. Under **state capitalism**, the government closely monitors and regulates the resources and means of production, which are privately owned.

- According to **Karl Marx**, capitalism brings workers and employers into conflict. The only way to resolve the conflict is workers' revolution to replace capitalism with **communism**.

- The economy is a quickly changing social institution. Economic trends include **globalization, demand for educated professionals, self-employment**, and **diversity in the workplace**.

Government

- The **government** is the institution entrusted with making and enforcing the rules of the society, as well as with regulating relations with other societies.

- Most of the world's governments fall into one of four categories: **monarchy, democracy, authoritarianism**, or **totalitarianism**.

- A **monarchy** is a political system in which a representative from one family controls the government and power is passed on through that family from generation to generation.

- A **democracy** is a political system in which the citizens periodically choose officials to run their government.

- **Authoritarianism** is a political system that does not allow citizens to participate in government.

- **Totalitarianism** is a political system under which the government maintains tight control over nearly all aspects of citizens' lives.

- The U.S. government is characterized by a **limited welfare state** and a **two-party political system**.

- Conflicts in governments generally take three forms: **revolution**, **war**, and **terrorism**.

Family

- The institution of **family** has three important functions: to provide for the rearing of children, to provide a sense of identity or belonging among its members, and to transmit culture between generations.

- There are two types of families. A **nuclear family** comprises a mother, father, and their children living under one roof. An **extended family** includes several generations and branches living nearby.

- **Marriage** is a foundation of family life. It exists in every society, with some variations.

- **Alternative families** such as single-parent households, unmarried couples, and gay and lesbian couples are on the rise in the United States.

Religion

- **Religion** is a social institution that answers our larger questions and explains the seemingly inexplicable.

- The world's major religions include **Christianity**, **Islam**, **Judaism**, **Hinduism**, and **Buddhism**.

- Religious groups include **churches**, **sects**, and **cults**.

- In the United States, social class, race, and ethnicity are factors in how religious a person is.

Education

- **Education** is the preparation of children for adulthood. It is an important agent of socialization and encourages social integration.

- The quality of education at public and private schools varies greatly in the United States.

Medicine

- The institution of **medicine** is responsible for defining and treating physical and mental illnesses among members of a society. The goal of a society's medical establishment is to promote **health**, the total well-being of its people.

- The definitions of physical and mental illnesses are different in different cultures.

- **Scientific medicine** is an approach to healing that focuses on illness. This method is common in the United States.

- **Holistic medicine** is an approach to healing that focuses on a patient's whole environment.

Social Groups and Organizations

- Groups, Aggregates, and Categories
- Group Classifications
- Social Integration
- Groups Within Society

4

Though individuality is positive and natural, we all need other people in our lives, and we form alliances with others every day. One of the most basic ways to arrange human beings is into groups. Large or small, groups serve many functions. They give an individual a sense of identity, as well as meet individual needs such as the need for emotional intimacy. In some groups, we have close personal ties to the other members. Other groups are so large and impersonal that we might never get to meet the other members. Some groups work to accomplish a task, and others meet just because the members feel a personal connection to one another.

As societies modernize, the sizes and purposes of groups change. In nonindustrialized societies, few groups exist, but in large, industrialized societies, residents commonly claim membership in a wide variety of groups. Because many types of society are so different from one another, it only makes sense that groups can differ widely in importance, purpose, and prevalence depending on the society in which they exist.

Groups, Aggregates, and Categories

Sociological study relies on the ability to classify the people being studied in order to arrive at correct conclusions. Classifications include groups, aggregates, and categories.

GROUPS

A **group** consists of two or more people who are distinct in the following three ways:

- Interact over time.

- Have a sense of identity or belonging.

- Have norms that nonmembers don't have.

> *EXAMPLE: A class of students is a group. Classes by definition consist of more than two people, meet at least a few times a week for an entire semester, and identify themselves on the basis of what classes they are taking. Students in a class must follow that professor's class and test schedule, as well as rules for behavior and contribution in class.*

Many different types of groups exist in industrialized societies, including school classes, social clubs, sports teams, neighborhood associations, religious communities, and volunteer organizations. Within any group, it is not uncommon for a few people to have an especially close relationship and form a **clique**, which is an internal cluster or faction within a group.

AGGREGATE

The word *group* is sometimes confused with the word *aggregate*. An **aggregate** is a collection of people who happen to be at the same place at the same time but who have no other connection to one another.

> *EXAMPLE: The people gathered in a restaurant on a particular evening are an example of an aggregate, not a group. Those people probably do not know one another, and they'll likely never again be in the same place at the same time.*

CATEGORY

A **category** is a collection of people who share a particular characteristic. They do not necessarily interact with one another and have nothing else in common.

> *EXAMPLE: Categories of people might include people who have green eyes, people who were born in Nevada, and women who have given birth to twins.*

Group Classifications

Humans have a natural tendency to form groups, and a single person can be a part of several groups at a time.

PRIMARY GROUPS AND SECONDARY GROUPS

A person can belong to several groups at once, but not all of those groups will be of the same importance or have the same effect or role in his or her life.

A **primary group** offers a great deal of intimacy. Members of a primary group meet the following criteria:

- Meet frequently on a face-to-face basis.
- Have a sense of identity or belonging that lasts a long time.
- Share little task orientation.
- Have emotional intimacy.

CHAPTER 4
SOCIAL GROUPS

A **secondary** group is more formal and less personal. Members of a secondary group meet the following criteria:

- Do not meet frequently, or they meet only for short periods of time.

- Share a sense of identity or belonging only until the group ends.

- Are task-oriented.

- Feel little emotional intimacy.

> EXAMPLE: *A family is an example of a primary group, and an after-school job in a fast-food restaurant is an example of a secondary group.*

Criterion	Family (primary group)	After-school job (secondary group)
Frequency of meeting	Every day for years or decades	Several hours a week, probably less or none if the person finds a different job
Duration of sense of identity	A lifetime, despite changes in composition (moving out, divorce, remarriage, or death)	Usually disappears when not at place of work
Task orientation	None. A person belongs to family simply by virtue of existence.	A person is there to accomplish a specific task and do his or her job.
Emotional intimacy	Strong. Family members see each other at their best and worst and are privy to one another's feelings.	It is inappropriate to show strong emotion or to discuss personal problems. Relationships are generally impersonal and work-related.

IN-GROUPS AND OUT-GROUPS

An **in-group** is a group to which we belong and to which we feel loyalty. An **out-group** is a group to which we do not belong and to which we feel no loyalty.

We judge people to be members of our group based on factors including religion, race, nationality, job category, and level of education. When we meet a person for the first time, we often size them up to see if they are "one of us." One person's perception of another to be a member of the same group can foment feelings of loyalty or shared identity. Individuals who meet by chance and happen to share something in common, such as their hometown or alma mater, often feel an immediate kinship.

> **Muslims As an Out-Group in the United States** *The perception that someone is a member of an out-group can lead to competition, discrimination, and even hatred. After the attacks of September 11, 2001, many people viewed followers of Islam as members of the out-group and developed an "us-and-them" attitude that vilified Muslims. The in-group became Americans who were not Muslim, and the out-group became members of the Muslim faith, regardless of nationality.*

CHAPTER 4
SOCIAL GROUPS

Labels and Out-Groups

Sometimes we perceive a person to be a member of an out-group and interpret his or her behaviors very differently from our own. Men may think of another man who strives to succeed professionally as being "ambitious," but they might label a woman who exhibits the same behaviors as being "pushy." The members of a particular religious background might consider themselves "secure" in their beliefs but call members of another religion "self-righteous" for demonstrating similar levels of certainty in their respective religions.

Identifying a group as an out-group can serve several functions. By pointing out a group that we are not part of, we increase our commitment to the groups of which we are members. If we claim that a particular out-group espouses beliefs that we disavow, we confirm our ideological compatibility with the groups to which we belong. By claiming that an out-group is bad, we are implying that, in comparison, our group is good.

REFERENCE GROUPS

The group to which we compare ourselves for purposes of self-evaluation is called a **reference group**.

> EXAMPLE: *Susan graduates from college and lands a job as a marketing assistant in a large corporation. To find out whether the proposed salary is fair, she can compare the offer against those of the other members of her graduating class or against the salaries of marketing assistants at similar corporations nationwide. Her reference groups would be her graduating class and all marketing assistants, respectively.*

Self-evaluation is largely a social phenomenon, in that we look for others with whom to compare ourselves. In our society, people compare themselves to others in similar age groups and with similar educational levels to determine how successful they are materially. If a person who rents an apartment sees that others of the same age and education own their own homes, his or her self-evaluation will be negative. On the other hand, if a person owns a home and a vacation home while his or her peers own only one home, his or her self-evaluation will be positive.

Specific Groups as Reference Groups

Primary or secondary groups can serve as a reference group.

- If we feel stymied in our career progress, we look to our best friends to see how they are doing and then evaluate ourselves in comparison to them.

- If we think that we should be paid more, we can look to other members of our company and see how much they are making.

A general category can also serve as a reference group. If a person worries about approaching thirty without being married, he or she can look at a general cross-section of thirty-year-olds to see whether the majority of them are married and adjust the self-assessment accordingly.

People often use celebrities as reference groups. If a woman wants to know whether she's slim enough and uses a supermodel as a reference, the answer will probably be no. If she compares herself to a more full-figured woman, the answer might be yes. A young man who aspires to a career in sports will compare his career progress to that of his favorite player and judge himself by how closely his career mirrors that of his idol.

Social Integration

Social integration is the degree to which an individual feels connected to the other people in his or her group or community.

DURKHEIM'S STUDY OF SUICIDE

The term *social integration* first came into use in the work of French sociologist **Émile Durkheim**. Durkheim wanted to understand why some people were more likely than others to take their own lives.

Durkheim's term for a lack of social integration was **anomie.** He concluded that three characteristics put some people at a higher risk of suicide than others, and that anomie was partly to blame:

- **Gender (male):** In most societies, men have more freedom and are more independent than women. While this might sound like a good thing, it can lead some men to feel that they have few significant relationships with other people and that it would be an admission of weakness to seek advice or comfort from others. This can lead to feelings of being cut off from a group or community.

- **Religion (Protestant):** Durkheim felt that Protestants were more likely to commit suicide than Catholics or Jews because the religious practices of the latter two religions emphasize the development of closer ties among their members. People who do not develop close ties with others are more likely to commit suicide.

- **Marital status (single):** Durkheim used the idea of social integration to explain the higher suicide rate among unmarried people. He concluded that people who were not married had fewer connections to other people and were less likely to feel part of the larger community.

Durkheim's connection of social integration to the suicide rate is still relevant today. People who attempt suicide are much more likely to say they feel lonely and isolated from others and claim to have few significant relationships, confirming what Durkheim hypothesized over one hundred years ago.

GROUP DYNAMICS

The term **group dynamics** implies that our thoughts and behaviors are influenced by the groups to which we belong and that, in turn, we influence how the group as a whole thinks and behaves.

> EXAMPLE: *Children's behavior is influenced by the behavior of other children. Clothing styles, speech patterns, and mannerisms spread quickly among groups of children. When a few children in a classroom begin using a particular expression, soon all the kids in the class will be using the same expression.*

This example illustrates two ways in which group dynamics work. First, one or two children adopt a mannerism and it spreads to the group. After the majority of the group has adopted it, it is very likely that other individual children will adopt it. Groups influence individuals, and individuals influence groups.

Adults are also influenced by the behavior of others. When adults voluntarily join a new group, they usually want to fit in and show others that they are worthy of membership. New members of a group are even more likely to be influenced by group dynamics because they don't want to seem obstinate or contrary. It usually takes a while before the new member is able to influence the thoughts and behavior of the group.

GROUP SIZE AND MEMBER INTERACTION

Georg Simmel was one of the first sociologists to look at how the size of a group affects interactions among its members. Simmel believed that in a **dyad**, a group of two people, interactions were intense and very personal. He also believed that a dyad was the least stable category of groups. A marriage is an example of a dyad. Simmel further said that a **triad**, a group of three people, was much more stable because conflicts between two of its members could be mediated by the third person. In general, Simmel believed that larger groups were more stable than smaller groups, but that in smaller groups the interactions between members were more intense and more intimate.

In the early 1950s, **Solomon Asch** conducted an experiment that illustrated how strongly group membership can influence behavior. He found that one-third of the subjects he tested were influenced by the group's consensus, even though the group was obviously incorrect.

Social Pressure To analyze the power of groups, Asch solicited students for a study of visual perception. Before the experiment began, he told all but one of the group of eight that the real purpose was to pressure the remaining person into going along with the group's decision. He showed the group two cards—one with one line, another with three lines of varying heights. The students were supposed to identify the line on the second card that was the same length as the line on the first card. The correct choice was easy to identify. Most students made the appropriate choice until Asch's accomplices began answering incorrectly. One third of all participants conformed to the group and answered incorrectly.

CHAPTER 4
SOCIAL GROUPS

GROUPTHINK

The sociologist **Irving Janis** coined the term **groupthink** to refer to the tendency of people in positions of power to follow the opinions of the group to the point that there is a narrow view of the issue at hand. When groupthink operates, the emerging viewpoint is that there is only one correct course of action and anyone who disagrees is labeled as disloyal.

> *EXAMPLE: President Franklin D. Roosevelt and his advisors concluded that the Japanese would never attack a U.S. installation. Some members of Roosevelt's inner circle felt differently but were not assertive in voicing their opinions, since they did not want to contradict the group consensus and appear disloyal. When the Japanese attacked Pearl Harbor on December 7, 1941, the general consensus was revealed to be incorrect.*

Groups Within Society

Each society is made up of smaller groups and associations that are built on social class, personal interest, or common goals.

THE POWER ELITE

Sociologist **C. Wright Mills** used the term **power elite** to refer to his theory that the United States is actually run by a small group representing the most wealthy, powerful, and influential people in business, government, and the military. According to Mills, their decisions dictate the policies of this country more than those of the voting public. Mills also pointed out that the influence of the power elite overlaps into many different areas. For example, a wealthy businessman may make large contributions to a particular political candidate.

VOLUNTARY ASSOCIATIONS

A **voluntary association** is a group that people choose to join, in which members are united by the pursuit of a common goal. Some voluntary associations operate on the local level, such as the parent-teacher organization at a particular school. Membership in any given PTA is voluntary, and the members unite to achieve the goal of encouraging communication between parents and teachers in the hope of benefiting local education.

Some voluntary associations operate on a statewide level, such as a campaign to reelect a particular state politician. Others function on a nationwide basis, such as the Girl Scouts or the National Association for the Advancement of Colored People (NAACP). Still others are international.

Voluntary associations can be temporary or permanent.

- In a temporary voluntary association, the group disbands once the common goal is achieved.

  EXAMPLE: *A voluntary association forms to protest a particular piece of legislation. The association dissolves once the law is repealed.*

- In a permanent voluntary association, the group exists as long as individuals are interested in belonging to it.

    EXAMPLE: Many individuals who join Alcoholics Anonymous remain active members for the rest of their lives.

FORMAL ORGANIZATIONS

A **formal organization** is a secondary group organized to achieve specific goals. Formal organizations tend to be larger and more impersonal than voluntary associations. There are many formal organizations in industrialized countries, but few exist in nonindustrialized societies.

    EXAMPLE: A corporation is usually a formal organization. Corporations tend to be large and are characterized by secondary relations among their employees. The goal of most corporations is very specific: to increase profits.

BUREAUCRACY

As identified by the sociologist **Max Weber**, a **bureaucracy** is a type of formal organization in which a rational approach is used to handle large tasks. Weber believed that as societies modernize, they become more rational, resulting in the creation of bureaucracies. As they industrialize, they grow larger, which means that the tasks to be accomplished become more numerous and complex.

Weber was convinced that bureaucracies would gain increasing power over modern life. Before long, almost every aspect of society would be governed by bureaucratic rules and regulations. Weber called this process the **rationalization of society**.

The Bureaucracy of Communication Before industrialization, communication was accomplished simply and most often in person or via messenger. Today, we must be able to communicate with members of our own society as well as those in other societies. One of the most popular communications media is the telephone. The amount of information transmitted over telephone lines through faxes, modems, and telephones is enormous, and the company entrusted to provide this service, the phone company, has become a classic example of a bureaucracy.

Characteristics of a Bureaucracy

According to Weber, a bureaucracy has several characteristics that distinguish it from other formal organizations.

1. **A bureaucracy is characterized by a division of labor.** In a bureaucracy, people specialize in the performance of one type of work. Using the phone company as an example, there are people who handle customers' bills, others who provide directory information, and others who climb the poles and repair the wires. The people who repair the wires do not handle customers' bills and vice versa.

2. **In a bureaucracy, there are written rules for how jobs are to be performed.** All jobs in a certain category must be performed exactly the same way, regardless of who is doing the work. All of the people who perform a specific job receive similar training, and the same standards for job performance are applied equally to everyone.

3. **Jobs are arranged in a hierarchy.** If the workplace were a pyramid, the top levels would represent upper management and the bottom levels would represent the rank-and-file workers. The top spot is usually occupied by a single person, while the bottom levels are occupied by an increasing number of jobs. Each level assigns tasks to the level below it, and each level reports to the level above it.

4. **Official communication is written down to minimize confusion and to facilitate the organization and maintenance of records.** Keeping written or electronic records documents the performance of individuals, departments, and the corporation as a whole. Communication is also written because it is more reliable

and not susceptible to an individual's memory lapses or inaccurate interpretation of information.

5. **Employees have an impersonal relationship with the organization.** The most important factors of a bureaucracy are the office and the job, not the individual doing the job. Each employee's loyalty should be to the organization, and not to the individual to whom they report.

Ideal Type

Weber's original concept of a bureaucracy represented an ideal type. An **ideal type** is a description of how an organization should ideally be run and is often very different from how it operates in reality. In Weber's view, if everyone did exactly as they were supposed to and no one deviated from their assigned tasks in any way, the bureaucracy would operate perfectly, and all goals would be accomplished. But in a complex bureaucracy, what exists on paper may bear little resemblance to reality.

Bureaucratic Goals

All bureaucracies have officially stated goals, which are sometimes called missions or objectives. One of the most common goals of all bureaucracies—usually unstated—is simply self-perpetuation. No bureaucratic organization wants to face extinction. When a bureaucracy's stated goals are met or prove to be unrealizable, the organization must come up with new goals in order to continue to exist. This is called *goal displacement* (sometimes called *goal replacement*). **Goal displacement** occurs when an organization displaces one goal with another in order to continue to exist.

EXAMPLE: The National Foundation for the March of Dimes was organized in the 1930s with the specific goal of eradicating polio. Approximately twenty years later, Dr. Jonas Salk developed a vaccine for the crippling disease, and the March of Dimes was faced with the bittersweet reality of having to admit that its mission had been accomplished. Rather than face extinction, however, the nonprofit organization displaced their original goal with a new one: the eradication of birth defects. Birth defects, in all their myriad forms, will probably never be totally eliminated, so the National Foundation for the March of Dimes will continue to exist for many years to come.

Networking

Bureaucracies and other formal organizations are often large and impersonal. Newcomers may be daunted when other members are unfamiliar, and the sheer size and complexity of the company can be disconcerting. In a vast organization, successful navigation requires the formation of networks. A **network** is a series of social ties that can be important sources of information, contacts, and assistance for its members.

EXAMPLE: Mary joins a large corporation as an accountant. At first, she feels like an outsider because she seems to have little in common with anybody, and she is one of only two female accountants in the company. She introduces herself to that accountant and they start having lunch together once a week. Soon, other female executives join in, and the size of the group increases. Eventually, female executives from other companies join the group, and an effective network emerges. They talk about changes in accounting law, workplace problems, and job opportunities. As time goes on, new members might be added to the network, and existing members might drop out. However, the network will continue to exist as long as there is a need for the information, contacts, and assistance it can provide.

Problems with Bureaucracies

Though bureaucracies can be efficient, many problems can hinder them.

On paper, bureaucracies appear to be the most rational approach to accomplishing stated goals, but human beings are not always rational.

- In formulating the ideal type bureaucracy, Weber did not allow for the inevitable formation of primary relationships, which are antithetical to the stated goals of a bureaucracy because loyalty shifts from the organization to the individual. Primary relationships tend to develop in bureaucracies because people feel a sense of **alienation**, or feelings that they are being treated as objects rather than people.

Sometimes the rules and regulations in a bureaucracy grow rigid to the point of inefficiency.

- If a person with a Ph.D. applies for a job as a college professor and is told to present his or her high school diploma as part of the required paperwork, the bureaucracy's regulations are too rigid and may hurt that bureaucracy's chances of hiring a quality employee.

In some bureaucracies, so much literal and figurative distance exists between the highest and the lowest ranks that the bureaucracy is rendered ineffective.

- In many corporations, those making the decisions have never actually done the work of the people their decisions affect, so their directives are either insufficient to solve the problems at hand or are ignored altogether. In an ideal bureaucracy, all directives are carried out exactly as they are issued. To do otherwise contributes to inefficiency.

Iron Law of Oligarchy

Sociologist **Robert Michels** theorized that bureaucracies tend to be run by a small group of people at the top, who he believed acted primarily out of self-interest, and who carefully controlled outsiders' access to power and resources. He called this the Iron Law of Oligarchy. The term **oligarchy** means the rule of many by the few.

Michels believed that top bureaucrats had a vested interest in maintaining the status quo, which benefited them most of all. He said that positions of power, as well as access to resources such as money, were passed among the members of the group, thereby excluding outsiders. When a U.S. president takes office, he usually awards top cabinet posts to people he knows or to those who have been loyal to him in the past. Though policies such as term limits and checks and balances are supposed to prevent an oligarchy from developing at the highest levels of government, a close examination of a sitting president's cabinet lends partial credence to Michels's theory. If oligarchies go too far, however, they run the risk of provoking a backlash among the very people they are trying to govern.

How do secondary groups evolve into primary groups and vice versa? What conflicts might arise from these changing relationships?

Primary groups are close, personal relationships based on emotional intimacy, whereas secondary groups are task-oriented, impersonal relationships. Secondary groups can evolve into primary groups, and primary groups can evolve into secondary groups, if the quality and quantity of the interaction changes. Conflicts may arise from these changing relationships when a person does not accept the changed nature of a group.

As the nature of interaction changes, secondary groups can evolve into primary groups. One example is of a person who starts a new job. When the new employee arrives on her first day of work, she probably does not know anyone. She is dependent on coworkers to explain the norms and procedures within the company. This dependence intensifies if the newcomer and her fellow employees spend a lot of time together. Sometimes people who work in the same organization have to travel together or entertain clients together. Coworkers automatically have a lot in common because they work at the same company. They often undergo work-related successes and failures together. Most people spend more time with coworkers than with their own families.

As time goes by, the person becomes more at ease and begins socializing with coworkers and developing stronger bonds of friendship. Ultimately, this newcomer may create a primary group with several close friends at work with whom she feels a strong connection. This group's discussions are no longer strictly work-related; the coworkers become comfortable discussing personal issues with each other.

Conflicts may arise in these new relationships when personal friendships hurt a business relationship. Even though coworkers have developed personal bonds, their overarching connection is as employees. The needs of the secondary group—to have work done on time, to make a profit, to reach a sales goal—may not be

Student Essay

compatible with the goals of the primary group. Camaraderie, emotional support, and a sense of belonging may or may not help meet the goals of the secondary group. Conflict arises when a primary group is forced to act like a secondary group.

Primary groups can also devolve into secondary relationships when a person leaves a job. The members no longer meet frequently on a face-to-face basis. They no longer share a sense of identity based on where they worked. The former coworkers may still occasionally get together for a social lunch, but their bond is no longer as close. College roommates, high-school friends, and former fraternity brothers also often experience this change in relationship status.

When a primary group becomes a secondary group, conflict may arise when one person does not accept the relationship's shift. A person can feel hurt and rejected when a close friend moves away and reduces contact, neglecting to make or return phone calls. Most people can read the signs of a changing relationship and behave accordingly, but occasionally two people's expectations are different, causing tension in the relationship.

Humans have a natural tendency to join groups. Over a lifetime, a person will belong to many groups, both primary and secondary groups. Conflict will occur when these relationships change. Understanding the nature of that conflict and examining expectations can help people navigate these situations.

Sample Test Questions

1. How do primary groups differ from secondary groups? Use examples from your own life to explain.

2. Have you ever been a member of a bureaucracy? How do you know it was a bureaucracy? Did it function as an ideal type?

3. What reference groups do you use? What kinds of comparisons do you make between the individuals in your reference groups and yourself? What are the problems with using this group as a reference group?

4. What are the positive and negative aspects of group dynamics?

5. Over 100 years ago, Durkheim identified three characteristics that made a person more vulnerable to committing suicide. What are these characteristics, and how applicable are they today?

6. People in a stadium watching a baseball game and people standing in line at the grocery checkout are examples of
   A. aggregrates
   B. groups
   C. categories
   D. cliques

7. What was Georg Simmel's contribution to the study of groups?
   A. He concluded that smaller groups are more stable than larger groups.
   B. He coined the term *groupthink*.
   C. He studied the effects of anomie on white, male Protestants.
   D. He looked at how the size of a group influences the interactions of its members.

8. *What was Solomon Asch's contribution to the study of groups?*
    A.   He analyzed how people's visual acuity can decline in a group.
    B.   He looked at how strongly group membership influences the ways we behave.
    C.   He theorized that dyads were more stable than triads.
    D.   He described the identifying characteristics of bureaucracies.

9. *Which of the following is NOT a common problem faced by bureaucracies?*
    A.   goal displacement
    B.   irrational human beings
    C.   inefficient hierarchies
    D.   lax rules and regulations

10. *According to C. Wright Mills, which of the following would be a member of the power elite?*
    A.   a first-year member of Congress
    B.   a lieutenant colonel in the Navy
    C.   Bill Gates
    D.   the head of the PTA

CHAPTER 4
SOCIAL GROUPS

ANSWERS

1. Primary groups differ from secondary groups in the quality, length, and breadth of the relationships. They also differ in their purposes. My primary groups are my family, my rowing team, and my online chat group. I'm close with my siblings and see them frequently—I even share an apartment with my older brother. Our relationship is based on friendship, without any other goal. I also spend many hours per week with the rowing team. Although our relationship began as a secondary group with the common goal of winning races, we have now become friends who do things together other than row. Even though I have never physically met the members of my online chat groups, we talk multiple times a day on a variety of subjects and have done so for over a year. My secondary groups are the student body and the workplace. I study best alone and don't have time to talk between classes. I don't like my job, so I spend as little time there as possible.

2. I spent one summer doing data entry for a national health-insurance company, a big bureaucracy. I knew it was a bureaucracy because everybody had a specific job to do, and there was no crossover between jobs. There was also a clear hierarchy; we all knew to whom each individual reported. On my first day, I was given a packet thirty pages long about all of the rules that existed, how to fill out time sheets, etc. It was not an ideal bureaucracy because many people bore loyalty to other people, rather than to the company, and others hated their supervisors and left the company because of them.

3. My main reference group is the people with whom I graduated high school. I compare myself to them in terms of what colleges we were accepted to, the colleges we decided to attend, what our majors are, and what kind of grades we make. One problem in using this group as a reference group is that the majority of the group are underachievers. Most of us selected colleges where we could succeed easily without having to learn much more than we did in high school. In relation to this group, I am successful, but these people are not representative of the general college population.

4. *Group dynamics* is the term that implies that our thoughts and behaviors are influenced by the groups we are members of and, in turn, we influence how the group as a whole thinks and behaves. When a group adopts a behavior that is socially acceptable or appropriate, such as following the rules of the road, then the group dynamic is a positive one. Sometimes, an individual driver can influence the group. For example, if you are driving on a highway and one person is braking or driving more slowly than the majority of the drivers, the group will slow down. Ultimately, the influence is positive, since there will be fewer accidents. The negative aspects of group dynamics include groupthink. One or two individuals may know that a decision is wrong or dangerous, but they go along with the group decision in order not to be ostracized.

5. According to Durkheim, the people most likely to commit suicide are those suffering from social isolation, or anomie. Most often, these people are single, male Protestants. These categories are still valid today. Men are four times more likely than women to commit suicide. Divorced, widowed, or otherwise single men are more likely to commit suicide than married men. This group includes elderly men whose wives have died. Protestants are more likely to commit suicide than Jews or Catholics because Protestants generally don't form communities as tightly knit as those of Jews and Catholics.

6. **A**

7. **D**

8. **B**

9. **D**

10. **C**

Summary

Groups, Aggregates, and Categories

- A **group** consists of two or more people who interact over time, have a sense of identity and belonging, and have norms that make them act differently from nonmembers.

- An **aggregrate** is a collection of people who just happen to be in the same place at the same time.

- A **category** is a collection of people who share a particular characteristic. They do not necessarily interact with one another and have nothing else in common.

Group Classifications

- **Primary groups** tend to be small and are characterized by emotional intimacy among members.

- **Secondary groups** tend to be larger and meet primarily for the purpose of accomplishing some kind of task.

- An **in-group** is a group to which we belong and to which we feel a sense of loyalty.

- An **out-group** is a one to which we don't belong and to which we don't feel a sense of loyalty.

- For purposes of self-evaluation, people often turn to **reference groups**. Reference groups can be either primary or secondary in nature, or they can be general categories or even celebrities.

Social Integration

- It's important to feel an emotional connection to one's group or to one's community. Such a feeling is called **social integration**.

- **Émile Durkheim** coined the term **anomie** to indicate a lack of social integration. He concluded that anomie was one factor in putting single, male Protestants at greater risk for suicide.

- Sociology also studies **group dynamics,** which is the term that implies that our thoughts and behaviors are influenced by the groups of which we are members. In turn, our thoughts and behaviors can influence those of other group members.

- **Georg Simmel** studied how group size affects interactions between group members. He found that a **dyad,** a group of two people, is less stable than a **triad,** a group of three people.

- **Irving Janis** coined the term **groupthink** to refer to the tendency of people in positions of power to follow the opinions of the group and to ignore any dissenting opinions.

Groups Within Society

- Each society is made up of smaller groups and associations.

- According to **C. Wright Mills**, the **power elite,** a small group representing the most powerful and influential people, runs the United States.

- A **voluntary association** is a group that we choose to join, in which the members are united by the pursuit of a common goal. These associations can be temporary or permanent.

- As societies modernize, groups change in size and purpose. A feature of modernized societies is the **formal organization,** a secondary group organized to achieve specific goals.

CHAPTER 4 SOCIAL GROUPS

- A **bureaucracy** is an example of a formal organization that arises as a result of modernization. Weber argued that bureaucracies gain increasing power over everyday life in a process called **rationalization of society.**

- A bureaucracy is characterized by a division of labor, written rules, hierarchy, official communication, and impersonal relationships within the organization.

- Bureaucracies appear to be the most rational approach to accomplishing the stated goals, but human beings are not always rational. This conflict makes bureaucracies inefficient.

- Sociologist **Robert Michels** theorized that bureaucracies tend to be run by an **oligarchy**, a small, ruling group.

Identity and Reality

5

- Social Construction of Reality
- Dramaturgy
- Social Status

There is no single, true universal reality. What is "real" differs from person to person, based on one's own ideas, circumstances, and knowledge. For example, a boy with a strict, stern father may not be happy when the father comes home. He may even try to avoid his father as much as possible. A boy with a more lenient and supportive father will be happy to see him and will eagerly seek his company. The reality of "father" for each of the boys, based on their social interactions, is quite different.

Each individual in a society has his or her own perceptions of reality, and that perception has a lot to do with social status. For example, in cultures where women have few legal rights and are not allowed to work outside the home, a wife may think she has a "good husband" simply because he does not beat her and allows her some freedom in pursuing her own interests. A wife working outside the home in an industrialized society may think she has a "bad husband" because he does not do enough housework. The way we create our own identities depends on how we create reality.

Social Construction of Reality

For centuries, philosophers and sociologists have pondered the idea of reality. Sociologists generally accept that reality is different for each individual.

The term **social construction of reality** refers to the theory that the way we present ourselves to other people is shaped partly by our interactions with others, as well as by our life experiences. How we were raised and what we were raised to believe affect how we present ourselves, how we perceive others, and how others perceive us. In short, our perceptions of reality are colored by our beliefs and backgrounds.

Our reality is also a complicated negotiation. What is real depends on what is socially acceptable. Most social interactions involve some acceptance of what's going on. While we participate in the construction of reality, it's not entirely a product of our own doing.

> *EXAMPLE: A wealthy individual, whose basic survival needs are met many times over, buys his pets gourmet, organic food that costs more per week than the weekly earnings of a minimum-wage worker. He is proud that he is able to take such good care of his animals and insists that it's the right thing to do if one really loves one's pets. After all, his vet was the one who recommended that he buy that brand. A minimum-wage worker who loads that food into the rich person's car might feel anger when he realizes how much money this individual spends on his pets. The minimum-wage worker might fume that this man's pets eat better than he does. He might wonder whether this rich man has any concept of reality.*

How we define everyday situations depends on our respective backgrounds and experiences. The wealthy individual has learned through interactions with others that spending money on one's pets is a worthy expense. His reality is one of pride. The minimum-wage worker has learned through interactions with others spending that much money on a pet is a negative thing, so his perception of the situation is entirely different.

THE THOMAS THEOREM

What is the "real" reality? Is buying a pet expensive food the right thing to do or a waste of money? According to sociologist **W. I. Thomas**, "if a person perceives a situation as real, it is real in its consequences." This statement is also known as the **Thomas Theorem.** In other words, our behavior depends not on the objective reality of a situation but on our subjective interpretation of reality. The consequences and results of behavior make it real. For example, a teenager who is defined as deviant might begin to act deviant. He makes his label real.

People perceive reality differently, and when they decide how they are going to view a person or a situation, they act accordingly. Since we all perceive reality differently, our reactions differ. Our definition of a situation as good or bad, to be embraced or avoided, dictates our response to it.

ETHNOMETHODOLOGY

Ethnomethodology, as founded by sociologist **Harold Garfinkel,** is a theory that looks at how we make sense of everyday situations. Though we may view a situation differently from those around us, our backgrounds provide us with some basic assumptions about everyday life. Ethnomethodology studies what those background assumptions are, how we arrive at them, and how they influence our perceptions of reality. In order to understand these assumptions, students of ethnomethodology are often taught to violate or challenge the taken-for-granted assumptions we have about everyday life.

> EXAMPLE: *In the United States, one background assumption is that emergency personnel, such as police officers, wear identifiable uniforms when on duty. An officer at an accident scene who is wearing everyday clothes might find that crowds won't obey someone who claims to be a police officer but is without a uniform. The officer might have difficulty keeping onlookers at bay or redirecting traffic away from the scene. When the background assumption is not fulfilled, members of the public will not respond as respectfully as they would if the officer were in uniform, and the officer will have a hard time performing required duties.*

CHAPTER 5
IDENTITY AND REALITY

Dramaturgy

Sociologist **Erving Goffman** developed the concept of **dramaturgy**, the idea that life is like a never-ending play in which people are actors. Goffman believed that when we are born, we are thrust onto a stage called everyday life, and that our socialization consists of learning how to play our assigned roles from other people. We enact our roles in the company of others, who are in turn enacting their roles in interaction with us. He believed that whatever we do, we are playing out some role on the stage of life.

Goffman distinguished between front stages and back stages. During our everyday life, we spend most of our lives on the front stage, where we get to deliver our lines and perform. A wedding is a front stage. A classroom lectern is a front stage. A dinner table can be a front stage. Almost any place where we act in front of others is a front stage. Sometimes we are allowed to retreat to the back stages of life. In these private areas, we don't have to act. We can be our real selves. We can also practice and prepare for our return to the front stage.

IMPRESSION MANAGEMENT

Goffman coined the term **impression management** to refer to our desire to manipulate others' impressions of us on the front stage. According to Goffman, we use various mechanisms, called **sign vehicles,** to present ourselves to others. The most commonly employed sign vehicles are the following:

- Social setting

- Appearance

- Manner of interacting

Social Setting

The social setting is the physical place where interaction occurs. It could be a doctor's examination room, a hallway, someone's home, or a professor's office. How we arrange our spaces, and what we put in them, conveys a lot of information about us. A person who lives in a huge home with security guards, attack dogs, and motion detectors conveys the message that he or she is very important, wealthy, and powerful, and probably that uninvited visitors should stay away. On the other hand, the owner of a house with no fence, lots of lights, and a welcome mat would seem much more inviting but perhaps not as rich or powerful.

How we decorate our settings, or what **props** we use, also gives clues to how we want people to think of us. A businesswoman with a photo of her family on her desk communicates that things outside of work are important in her life. When a professor displays her degrees and certificates on the wall of her office, she communicates that she wants to be viewed as a credible authority in her chosen field. When people decorate offices, hang pictures in clinics, or display artwork in their homes, they are using props to convey information about how they want others to see them.

Appearance

Our appearance also speaks volumes about us. People's first impressions are based almost exclusively on appearance.

- **Clothing:** The clothing we wear tells others whether we are rich or poor, whether we take care of ourselves, whether we have a job, and whether we take it seriously. Props such as a wedding band, a doctor's stethoscope, or a briefcase tell others even more about us.

- **Physical stature:** American society is obsessed with thinness, especially for women, and people often equate thinness with attractiveness. People commonly make assumptions about a person's personality and character based solely on his or her weight. The tendency to assume that a physically attractive person also possesses other good qualities is called the **halo effect**. For example, thin and attractive people are assumed to be smarter, funnier, and more self-controlled, honest, and efficient than their less thin and attractive peers. Conversely, we tend to think that heavier people lack self-discipline and are more disorganized than their thinner counterparts.

- **Race:** Anthropologically speaking, there are only three races: white, black, and Asian. Humans feel the need to assign every individual to one of the three races and then draw conclusions about their musical preferences, tastes in food, and home life based on that classification.

- **Stereotypes:** Many of the assumptions we make about people based on physical characteristics are actually stereotypes. A **stereotype** is an assumption we make about a person or group that is usually based on incomplete or inaccurate information. An individual or two may indeed fit a stereotype, but the danger is assuming that all people who share a particular characteristic are inherently the same.

Manner of Interacting

According to Goffman, our manner of interacting is also a sign vehicle. Our **manner of interacting** consists of the attitudes we convey in an attempt to get others to form certain impressions about us. One of the most common ways to convey attitudes is through nonverbal communication, the ways we have of communicating that do not use spoken words. These consist of gestures, facial expressions, and body language.

- **Gestures:** In our society, we often shake hands when we meet someone for the first time. The offer to shake hands signals that we want to meet the other individual, so when one person extends his or her right hand and the other person does not do likewise, the second person is insulting the first. Messages in gestures can be more subtle, as well. A person whose handshake is firm conveys confidence, but an individual with an intentionally crushing handshake is, in effect, claiming strength and domination over the other person.

- **Facial expressions:** Facial expressions also convey information. Humans can convey a surprising amount of information in a look or an expression: a smile, frown, grimace, raised eyebrows, and narrowed eyes all convey distinctly different messages.

- **Body language:** Our body language can also convey a wealth of meaning. Body language consists of the ways in which we use our bodies consciously and unconsciously to communicate. Most people are familiar with the body language that accompanies traditional mating rituals in our society. Sometimes body language gives clearer indications of a person's thoughts or feelings than words do. For example, if a person claims not to be upset by a recent romantic breakup but his or her movements and facial expressions lack their usual animation and energy, the individual's body language is contradicting his or her stated emotions.

PERSONAL SPACE

The way we command space is also a function of how we choose to present ourselves. **Personal space** refers to the area immediately around the body that a person can claim as his or her own. Like so many aspects of culture, the amount of personal space an individual claims differs from culture to culture. In general, residents of the West stand at least three or four feet away from the people they are speaking to. In parts of the Middle East, people tend to stand only about two feet away when conversing.

In general, the more intimate we are with a person, the closer we allow him or her to stand to us.

- 1–2 feet: Close friends, lovers, and family members
- 2–4 feet: Acquaintances and coworkers
- 4–12 feet: Formal acquaintances, such as a potential employer during a job interview

When someone stands closer than the culture deems appropriate, discomfort results because that person has invaded the accepted personal space. Powerful and prestigious people can command more personal space and in general are also more likely to invade others' personal space.

CHAPTER 5
IDENTITY AND REALITY

Social Status

The ways we choose to present ourselves to other people also give clues as to our **social status**, which is the position we occupy in a particular setting. In a doctor's office, the doctor occupies one status, the nurse another, and the receptionist still another. Some statuses carry more prestige and power than others. In our society, the status of doctor is more prestigious than the status of nurse, and the status of nurse is more prestigious than that of receptionist.

Statuses also exist in the home, including the positions of mother, father, oldest child, youngest child, and grandparent. Most of us occupy a number of different statuses in our lives. The collection of all of our different statuses from every setting is called our **status set**.

STATUS SYMBOLS

Sometimes we wear **status symbols**, or signs or symbols of a respective status. Professors wear academic regalia to identify their status within the collegiate setting. Successful businesspeople may drive luxurious cars or wear expensive clothing or jewelry to indicate a high financial status within the community. A wedding ring is also an example of a status symbol in our culture, as it communicates the message that the wearer is married.

Not all status symbols are positive. In some states, an individual who has been convicted of driving a car while intoxicated must put a bumper sticker saying "DUI" (Driving Under the Influence) or "Convicted DUI" on their car. The bumper sticker indicates a status that is generally looked down on in our society.

STATUS INCONSISTENCY

We tend to have more than one status at any given point in our lives, and most of the time there is consistency among our various statuses. Status inconsistency results when a person occupies one or more statuses that do not ordinarily coincide in the same person. A seventy-five-year-old grandmother who is a college freshman and a cab driver who is a classically trained Shakespearean actor both exhibit status inconsistency.

MASTER STATUS

A **master status** overrides all other statuses and becomes the one by which we are first known to others. For many people, their occupation is their master status, since it conveys so much about their income, education, skills, and interests. People who differ from the rest of society in some way may have a different master status. For many people who are homosexual, their sexual orientation becomes their master status, and others think of it when they hear those people's names. Their statuses as professionals, athletes, family members, and community leaders are secondary to their status as homosexuals.

> *Master Statuses in Global Cultures* In cultures where women are not afforded as many opportunities as men, their gender is their master status. In much of the United States, it could be argued that a minority person's race or ethnicity is a master status. Other master statuses could be celebrity, wealth, or having a physical disfigurement. Regardless of all of the other statuses a person may hold, the status that is immediately apparent to others makes the biggest impression and affects others' perceptions of that individual.

STIGMAS

Some of the traits we possess are actually stigmas. According to Goffman, a **stigma** is a trait or characteristic we possess that causes us to lose prestige in the eyes of others. A disfigured face might be a stigma, as someone whose face is severely disfigured is likely to have lost prestige among his or her peers and coworkers. Many would also consider homosexuality to be a stigmatizing characteristic. Because of widespread homophobia, many people would think less of a person they knew to be homosexual.

Goffman believed that a stigma that is permanent, severe, or both can cause an individual to have a **spoiled identity**, and others will always cast them in a negative light.

> EXAMPLE: *Convicted felons have a spoiled identity. Not only is their status as felons their master status, but it is a stigma so negative that it is likely that society will always think of them as convicted felons. Being a convicted felon is so stigmatizing that individuals will always be thought of as criminals even if they've served time and have been rehabilitated.*

DEGRADATION CEREMONIES

If an individual's identity is spoiled beyond redemption, sometimes the groups to which he or she belongs must decide how to handle his or her new identity. One way to deal with individuals whose identities have been spoiled is through a degradation ceremony. According to **Harold Garfinkel**, a **degradation ceremony** is a ritual designed to expel a person from a group and to strip this person of his or her identity as a group member.

There are several elements of a successful degradation ceremony:

1. The individual's stigma or transgression must be made known to the entire group.

2. An authority figure must make the individual's stigma known to the group. Group members cannot denounce one another.

3. The group must believe that the authority figure is acting out of concern for the whole group. If the group believes that the leader is denouncing an individual because of a personal feud or vendetta, the degradation ceremony will not be successful.

CHAPTER 5
IDENTITY AND REALITY

4. The transgressor must be criticized in public, before the entire group. This serves to further humiliate the guilty party and reinforce the boundaries of behavior to the rest of the group. By publicly denouncing a group member, the leader is also telling everyone what kinds of behavior will and will not be tolerated.

5. The offending individual must be evicted from the group. If the group leader allows the transgressor to remain in the group, he or she is communicating to the other members that bearing a stigma, or breaking the rules, will be tolerated.

CHAPTER 5
IDENTITY AND REALITY

**Was President Bill Clinton's 1998 impeachment a
degradation ceremony, according to Garfinkel's definition?
Your essay should present a clear argument.**

In many ways, President Clinton's impeachment in 1998
resembled a degradation ceremony. According to Harold Garfinkel,
a degradation ceremony is a ritual designed to expel from a group
a person with a spoiled identity and to strip that person of his
identity as a group member. Clinton's impeachment came close to
expelling the president from his group—and his job—but
ultimately failed.

To understand Clinton's impeachment as a degradation
ceremony, we must first identify in what ways it did resemble a
degradation ceremony. One of the first elements of a successful
degradation ceremony is making the individual's stigma or
transgression known to the entire group. This event definitely
occurred. In September 1998 independent counsel Kenneth Starr
presented his 445-page report to the House of Representatives
alleging eleven impeachable offenses that the president committed.
Within days, the House Judicial Committee released to the public
the sexually explicit Starr Report, and it became one of the most
downloaded documents on the internet.

Another important element of a degradation ceremony is that
the transgressor must be criticized in public, before the entire
group. In December 1998, the House of Representatives voted to
impeach the president. In early 1999 his trial began in the Senate.
In both instances, much of the debate and trial was televised.
Members of Congress criticized Clinton and his behavior. They
tried to humiliate him and to reinforce the appropriate boundaries
of behavior.

While Clinton's impeachment certainly contained elements of a
degradation ceremony, it did not ultimately meet all of Garfinkel's
criteria for one. The authority figure who makes public the
transgressor's behavior must be acting out of concern for the
whole group, and many Americans believed that Kenneth Starr,

Student Essay

designated as independent, was not in fact impartial. Many Americans also believed that Republicans in Congress were pursuing Clinton because of a partisan vendetta. First Lady Hillary Clinton referred to the investigation as a "vast right-wing conspiracy" against the president. Rather than acting out of concern for all Americans, the Republicans were trying to increase their own power by stigmatizing the president and eroding his authority.

One could argue that the Republicans would not have continued to pursue impeachment if the president had done what they wanted. They wanted the president to confess his sins, another crucial element in a degradation ceremony. But Clinton never explicitly acknowledged his transgression. In January 1998 he emphatically told the White House press corps, "I did not have sexual relations with that woman. . . . These allegations are false." Even after testifying before the grand jury, Clinton would not give the Republicans the public admission of guilt they wanted. He said that he had "misled people," including his wife, but he denied that he had lied or had asked others to lie on his behalf.

Ultimately, one cannot view Clinton's impeachment as a successful degradation ceremony because he was not evicted from the group. The Senate acquitted him, and Clinton served out the remainder of his term. Clinton was marginalized in the 2000 presidential election; no Democratic candidate wanted his support. By 2004, however, Clinton was back in the public eye. His lengthy autobiography, *My Life*, was an international bestseller. He campaigned actively for John Kerry, the Democratic presidential candidate. In early 2005 he regained his status as an international statesman when he worked with former president George H. W. Bush to coordinate relief efforts for the victims of the tsunami that swept through Southeast Asia.

Sample Test Questions

1. Compare and contrast ethnomethodology and the Thomas Theorem.

2. Create an ethnomethodological experiment to identify background assumptions. What will you do, what assumptions will you be testing, and what predictions can you make?

3. In what ways do we manage people's impressions of us? Imagine that you are a male college senior who looks and dresses like a snowboarder. If you were trying to get a job at a bank, how might you try to manage others' impressions of you?

4. What is the connection between appearance and status?

5. How does gender inform personal space?

6. Shakespeare famously wrote that "All the world's a stage." Which of the following people would be the most likely to agree with him?
   A. Harold Garfinkel
   B. Carol Gilligan
   C. Erving Goffman
   D. W. I. Thomas

7. Which of the following does the Thomas Theorem posit?
   A. Consequences make something real.
   B. Reality is a performance.
   C. We want to manage people's impressions of us.
   D. Stigmas can spoil reality.

8. Which of the following would Harold Garfinkel view as the best way to identify background assumptions?
   A. Take a course on ethnomethodology.
   B. Attend a play and then meet the actors backstage.
   C. Cheat on a test.
   D. Stand backward in an elevator and see how people react.

9. *A wedding band is an example of a*
    A. status symbol
    B. stigma
    C. stereotype
    D. master status

10. *A severe stigma can be a person's*
    A. status set
    B. stereotype
    C. master status
    D. halo effect

ANSWERS

1. According to both theories, reality is a social construction. Garfinkel's work focused on how people make sense of their surroundings. He hypothesized that people respond differently to the same situation based on their background assumptions. His goal was to identify these assumptions and determine how they influence our perceptions of reality. Thomas theorized that if people defined situations as real, then they were real in their consequences. He did not search for background assumptions but instead focused on how people turned assumptions into reality.

2. For my experiment, I will test people's assumptions about politeness. I will act in a manner contrary to normal behavior. Whenever someone asks me a polite question, I will answer it honestly. For example, when people ask me, "How are you?" I will not answer, "Fine, how are you?" I will tell them how I really feel at that moment and record their reaction. I predict that people will be surprised at my answer. They may initially respond as if I had given the expected response, because they may need time to process my unexpected answer.

3. According to Goffman, we manage others' impressions of us by manipulating sign vehicles. The most common sign vehicles are setting, appearance, and manner of interacting. In order to get a job at a bank, I would have to focus on two of Goffman's sign vehicles: appearance and manner. I can't really dictate the setting. I would cut my hair, shave my face, and wear a dark suit. I would also probably carry a leather briefcase. I would also pay attention to my body language. I would shake hands firmly and maintain eye contact.

4. According to Goffman, appearance is one of the sign vehicles that people manipulate in order to manage others' impressions. As we change our appearance, we change people's view of us. Appearance is also an important indication of status. We wear status symbols to convey our status. When we change our appearance, we change which status we are highlighting. For example, a female executive wearing a suit conveys a status of power and importance. When she changes into jeans and a

sweatshirt to attend her son's soccer game, she is emphasizing her status as a mother.

5.   When someone stands closer to us than our culture deems appropriate, we feel uncomfortable because they have invaded our personal space. Powerful and prestigious people, often men, can command more personal space and in general are also more likely to invade others' personal space. When a man stands closer to a woman than might be deemed culturally appropriate, he may be trying to intimidate or threaten her, conveying the message that he is more powerful than she is. It could also be interpreted as a sign of sexual interest. When women, who are generally less physically powerful than men, stand too close to a man, their behavior is more likely to be interpreted as a sexual overture than as a sign of power.

6. **C**

7. **A**

8. **D**

9. **A**

10. **C**

Summary

Social Construction of Reality

- The **social construction of reality** refers to the theory that the way we present ourselves to others is shaped by our interactions with others.

- The **Thomas Theorem** posits that if a person perceives a situation as real, it is real in its consequences. People will act according to how they perceive a person or a situation.

- **Ethnomethodology**, as founded by **Harold Garfinkel**, looks at how people make sense out of everyday situations by examining their background assumptions.

Dramaturgy

- **Erving Goffman** developed **dramaturgy**, the theory that all social life is like a drama or play in which everyone plays a role.

- Goffman coined the term **impression management** to refer to our desire to manipulate others' impressions of us.

- To manage impressions, we use three **sign vehicles: setting**, **appearance**, and **manner**.

- People also manage impressions by managing their **personal space**, the immediate area surrounding their body.

Social Status

- **Social status** is the position that we occupy in a particular setting.

- **Status symbols** are obvious signs or symbols of a respective status. They can be positive or negative.

- **Status inconsistency** occurs when a person occupies one or more statuses that do not usually coincide in a single person.

- **Master status** overrides all other statuses and is the one by which we are first known to others. For many people, their occupation is their master status.

- **Stigma** is Goffman's term for a trait or characteristic we possess that causes us to lose prestige in others' eyes.

- When stigma is permanent or severe, it can result in **spoiled identity**. People think negatively of those with spoiled identities.

- One way to deal with people with spoiled identities is through a **degradation ceremony**, a ritual designed to expel a person from a group.

Deviance

6

In the latter part of 2000, Houston-based Enron Corporation claimed that it had lost more than $500 million and filed for bankruptcy. An investigation revealed that Enron's accounting firm, Arthur Andersen, had reported artificially inflated earning figures and hidden Enron's debts, which amounted to hundreds of millions of dollars. Thousands of Enron workers lost their jobs and millions in retirement savings. Overall responsibility for the financial debacle fell on the shoulders of two people: Andrew Fastow (CFO) and Kenneth Lay (Chairman and CEO).

Fastow and Lay, two wealthy white men who did not commit a violent crime, don't seem to fit the label *deviant*. However, Fastow and Lay did violate the norms of society. Sociologists can use these men and their behavior to illustrate how definitions of deviance vary between cultures and between societies—even between communities—and how consequences for deviant behavior can vary depending on many factors.

What Is Deviance?

The word *deviance* connotes odd or unacceptable behavior, but in the sociological sense of the word, **deviance** is simply any violation of society's norms. Deviance can range from something minor, such as a traffic violation, to something major, such as murder.

Each society defines what is deviant and what is not, and definitions of deviance differ widely between societies. For example, some societies have much more stringent rules regarding gender roles than we have in the United States, and still other societies' rules governing gender roles are less stringent than ours.

> **Gender and Deviance** In the United States, women who cry in public in response to emotional situations are not generally considered deviant—even women who cry frequently and easily. This view of women has remained relatively constant. Over the past fifty years, however, society's perception of men who cry has changed. A man who cried publicly in the 1950s would have been considered deviant. Today, men who cry in response to extreme emotional situations are acting within society's norms. Male politicians cry when announcing defeat, male athletes cry after winning a championship, and male actors cry after winning an award. By today's standards, none of these men is committing a deviant act.

RELATIVISM AND DEVIANCE

Deviance is a relative issue, and standards for deviance change based on a number of factors, including the following:

- **Location:** A person speaking loudly during a church service would probably be considered deviant, whereas a person speaking loudly at a party would not. Society generally regards taking the life of another person to be a deviant act, but during wartime, killing another person is not considered deviant.

- **Age:** A five-year-old can cry in a supermarket without being considered deviant, but an older child or an adult cannot.

- **Social status:** A famous actor can skip to the front of a long line of people waiting to get into a popular club, but a nonfamous person would be considered deviant for trying to do the same.

- **Individual societies:** In the United States, customers in department stores do not try to negotiate prices or barter for goods. In some other countries, people understand that one should haggle over the price of an item; *not* to do so is considered deviant.

> *Cultural Norms and Deviance* In Japan, there are strict norms involving the exchange of business cards. One person presents his or her business card with the writing facing the recipient, who looks at it for a moment and asks a question about some of the information on the card. The question may be irrelevant, but it tells the giver that the recipient has read the card and acknowledges the person and his or her company. A Japanese executive who receives a business card and does not take the time to look at it and ask a question would be considered deviant.

Deviant Traits

A person does not need to act in a deviant manner in order to be considered deviant. Sometimes people are considered deviant because of a trait or a characteristic they possess. Sociologist **Erving Goffman** used the term **stigma** to identify deviant characteristics. These include violations of the norms of physical ability or appearance. For example, people who are confined to wheelchairs or who have IQs over 140 are deviant because they do not represent the usual behaviors or characteristics of most people.

SOCIAL CONTROL

Punishing people for deviant behavior reminds people what is expected of them and what will happen if they do not conform to society's norms. Every society has methods of **social control**, or means of encouraging conformity to norms (see Chapter 1). These methods of social control include positive sanctions and negative sanctions. A **positive sanction** is a socially constructed

expression of approval. A **negative sanction** is a socially constructed expression of disapproval.

Positive Sanctions

Society uses positive sanctions to reward people for following
norms. Positive sanctions can be formal, such as an award or a
raise. They can also be informal and include words, gestures, or
facial expressions.

> EXAMPLE: *The smile that a mother gives her child when he
> says "thank you" is a positive sanction.*

A reaction to an individual's actions can be a positive sanction,
even if it is not intended to be.

> EXAMPLE: *If a three-year-old learns a four-letter word at day
> care and says it to her parents, they might giggle and tell the
> child not to say it anymore. But the child repeats it because
> she likes seeing them laugh. Without realizing it, the girl's
> parents positively sanction her actions by laughing when she
> says her new word. Even though what they said was
> intended to discourage her, their actions conveyed the oppo-
> site meaning.*

Negative Sanctions

Like positive sanctions, negative sanctions can range from formal
to informal.

> EXAMPLE: *A speeding ticket or a prison sentence is a formal
> negative sanction. A raised eyebrow or a stare is an informal
> negative sanction.*

Some subcultures dole out negative sanctions for behaviors generally condoned by the rest of society. In our society, academic
achievement is usually held in high esteem. But in some subcultures, succeeding in a way that the dominant society approves of
is not considered a good thing. In some gangs, getting good
grades is not acceptable, and gang members who do well in
school are criticized by their friends for "selling out." Conformity
to traditional figures of authority, such as teachers, is negatively
sanctioned.

Symbolic Interactionist Perspective

Sociologists use a variety of theoretical perspectives to make sense of the world. These perspectives or theories provide a framework for understanding observations on topics such as deviance. The **symbolic interactionist perspective** of sociology views society as a product of everyday social interactions of individuals. Symbolic interactionists also study how people use symbols to create meaning. In studying deviance, these theorists look at how people in everyday situations define deviance, which differs between cultures and settings.

THEORY OF DIFFERENTIAL ASSOCIATION

Sociologist **Edwin Sutherland** studied deviance from the symbolic interactionist perspective. The basic tenet of his **theory of differential association** is that deviance is a learned behavior—people learn it from the different groups with which they associate. His theory counters arguments that deviant behavior is biological or due to personality. According to Sutherland, people commit deviant acts because they associate with individuals who act in a deviant manner.

He further explained exactly what one learns from people who commit deviance. He said that the future deviant learns values different from those of the dominant culture, as well as techniques for committing deviance.

> EXAMPLE: *In a gang environment, current gang members resocialize new members to norms that oppose those of the dominant culture. From the gang, these new members learn that stealing, carrying a gun, and using drugs are acceptable behaviors, whereas they were not before. In the meantime, the norms they learned at home are no longer acceptable within the gang environment, and they must reject those norms and values to accept the new ones. Current gang members also teach new members how to commit specific deviant acts, such as hotwiring a car or breaking into a home.*

Part of Sutherland's theory is that if people learn deviance from others, the people with whom we associate are of utmost importance. The closer the relationship, the more likely someone is to be influenced. Parents who worry that their children are socializing with an undesirable crowd have a justified concern.

> **EXAMPLE:** *If an adolescent changes schools and his new peer group smokes marijuana, the new student is more likely to smoke marijuana. On the other hand, if a student moves to a new school where no one smokes marijuana, he is less likely to take up the habit.*

Deviant Subcultures

When individuals share a particular form of deviance, they often form a **deviant subculture**, a way of living that differs from the dominant culture and is based on that shared deviance. Within the deviant subculture, individuals adopt new norms and values and sometimes feel alienated from the larger society. They end up relying more on the group to which they feel they most belong. When an individual becomes a member of a deviant subculture, the members of his immediate group often become his primary source of social interaction. The deviant feels comfortable among others who have also been rejected from the dominant society.

> **EXAMPLE:** *People released from prison often find that the dominant society does not welcome them back with open arms, and they often drift toward other ex-convicts to attain a sense of belonging and purpose, thereby forming a subculture. This deviant subculture helps to explain why rates of recidivism, or repeated offenses by convicted criminals, are so high. The ex-convict subculture sanctions and encourages further acts of deviance.*

CONTROL THEORY

Sociologist **Walter Reckless** developed the control theory to explain how some people resist the pressure to become deviants. According to **control theory**, people have two control systems that work against their desire to deviate. Each person has a set of inner controls and outer controls.

- **Inner controls** are internalized thought processes such as a sense of morality, conscience, or religious beliefs. People may also refrain from doing acts of deviance because they fear punishment or couldn't live with the guilt that would come from acting outside of society's norms. Inner controls represent a sort of internalized morality.

- **Outer controls** consist of the people in our lives who encourage us not to stray. They could be family members, police officers, clergy, or teachers. Whoever they are, they influence us to conform to society's expectations. A person who is tempted to engage in a deviant act can resist the temptation by imagining how others would react to his or her behavior.

Travis Hirschi and Control Theory

Sociologist **Travis Hirschi** elaborated on the control theory. He identified four elements that would render an individual more or less likely to commit deviance: attachment, commitment, involvement, and belief.

- **Attachment:** People who feel a strong attachment to other people, such as family or close friends, are less likely to be deviant. If people have weak relationships, they feel less need to conform to the other person's or group's norms. They are more likely to commit a deviant act.

- **Commitment:** Individuals who have a sincere commitment to legitimate goals are more likely to conform to society's norms. Those goals could be a legitimate job, higher education, financial stability, or a long-term relationship. When people have little confidence in the future, they are more likely to engage in deviance.

- **Involvement:** The more involved people are with legitimate activities, the less likely they are to deviate from appropriate behavior. A person with a job, a family, and membership in several clubs or organizations is less likely to commit deviance. Not only does he not have time to waste in potentially harmful activities, but he has a lot to lose if he does.

**CHAPTER 6
DEVIANCE**

- **Belief:** An individual who shares the same values as the dominant society, such as respect for authority, the importance of hard work, or the primacy of the family, is less likely to commit deviance. Individuals whose personal belief systems differ from those of the dominant society are more likely to commit deviance. A person raised to believe that it is acceptable to cheat, lie, and steal will probably not integrate into mainstream society as well as someone whose beliefs conform to the values of the larger society.

LABELING THEORY

A key aspect of the symbolic interactionist perspective of deviance is labeling theory. First proposed by sociologist **Howard Becker** in the 1960s, **labeling theory** posits that deviance is that which is so labeled. No status or behavior is inherently deviant until other people have judged it and labeled it deviant.

> _EXAMPLE: Some parents absolutely prohibit physical punishment of children, such as spanking, while other parents regularly use physical punishment to enforce household rules. Are parents who spank their children deviant? The answer depends on what is considered acceptable behavior within that given household, or within the greater society in which the family lives. Though spanking is inherently neither right nor wrong, it is subject to the often harsh judgment of others._

Primary and Secondary Deviance

Sociologist **Edwin Lemert** differentiated between primary deviance and secondary deviance. The difference between primary deviance and secondary deviance is in the reactions other people have to the original act of deviance.

Primary deviance is a deviant act that provokes little reaction and has limited effect on a person's self-esteem. The deviant does not change his or her behavior as a result of this act.

> EXAMPLE: *An adolescent who smokes cigarettes with other adolescents is not at risk of being labeled a deviant among her peers, since they all smoke. Even though adolescents who smoke cigarettes are considered deviant by the larger American society, that teenager's actions go relatively unnoticed, unpunished, and therefore unchanged. The primary deviance is of little consequence.*

Secondary deviance includes repeated deviant behavior that is brought on by other people's negative reactions to the original act of primary deviance.

> EXAMPLE: *The same adolescent moves to a new school where his peers never smoke and where smoking is considered a deviant behavior. The students call him names and exclude him from all of their social activities. Because of their reactions to his smoking, he feels like an outcast and begins to smoke more, perhaps engaging in other deviant activities, such as alcohol or drugs.*

According to Lemert, the reactions to the adolescent's primary deviance provoked a form of secondary deviance. Because his alleged friends reacted so negatively to his behavior, he began to engage in more of the deviant behavior. This repeated deviance results in the adolescent having a deviant identity. He now has a "reputation," and no one looks at him in quite the same way as before.

Chambliss and the Saints and Roughnecks

In the 1970s, sociologist **William Chambliss** studied two groups of high school boys to find out how strongly labels affected them. The eight boys in the group Chambliss called the Saints came from middle-class families. Society expected them to do well in life. The six boys in the other group, the Roughnecks, came from lower-class families in poorer neighborhoods. The community generally expected them to fail. Both groups engaged in deviant behavior—skipping school, fighting, and vandalizing property—but suffered different consequences. The teachers, the police, and the community excused the Saints' behavior because they believed the Saints were good boys overall. The same people saw the Roughnecks as bad and prosecuted them for their behavior more often.

Years later, all but one of the Saints had gone to college and subsequently into professional careers. Two Roughnecks went to college on athletic scholarships, graduated, and became coaches. Two never graduated from high school, and the other two ended up in prison.

Chambliss discovered that the boys' social class had much to do with the public's perception of them and the ways the public perceived their acts of deviance. He also hypothesized that a deviant label can become a self-fulfilling prophecy. The Roughnecks had heard for so long that they were never going to amount to much that they behaved in accordance with the negative expectations others had of them.

Structural Functional Theory

Another framework sociologists use to understand the world is the **structural functional theory**. Its central idea is that society is a complex unit, made up of interrelated parts. Sociologists who apply this theory study social structure and social function. French sociologist **Émile Durkheim** based his work on this theory.

FUNCTIONS OF DEVIANCE

Durkheim argued that deviance is a normal and necessary part of any society because it contributes to the social order. He identified four specific functions that deviance fulfills:

1. **Affirmation of cultural norms and values:** Seeing a person punished for a deviant act reinforces what a society sees as acceptable or unacceptable behavior. Sentencing a thief to prison affirms our culturally held value that stealing is wrong. Just as some people believe that the concept of God could not exist without the concept of the devil, deviance helps us affirm and define our own norms.

2. **Clarification of right and wrong:** Responses to deviant behavior help individuals distinguish between right and wrong. When a student cheats on a test and receives a failing grade for the course, the rest of the class learns that cheating is wrong and will not be tolerated.

3. **Unification of others in society:** Responses to deviance can bring people closer together. In the aftermath of the attacks on September 11, 2001, people across the United States, and even the world, were united in their shock and grief. There was a surge in patriotic feeling and a sense of social unity among the citizens of the United States.

4. **Promoting social change:** Deviance can also encourage the dominant society to consider alternative norms and values. Rosa Parks's act of deviance in Montgomery, Alabama, in 1955 led to the U.S. Supreme Court's declaration that segregation on public transportation was unconstitutional.

STRAIN THEORY OF DEVIANCE

Sometimes people find that when they attempt to attain culturally approved goals, their paths are blocked. Not everyone has access to **institutionalized means**, or legitimate ways of achieving success. **Strain theory**, developed by sociologist **Robert Merton**, posits that when people are prevented from achieving culturally approved goals through institutional means, they experience strain or frustration that can lead to deviance. He said that they also experience **anomie**, or feelings of being disconnected from society, which can occur when people do not have access to the institutionalized means to achieve their goals.

> EXAMPLE: *In a class of graduating high school seniors, 90 percent of the students have been accepted at various colleges. Five percent do not want to go to college, and the remaining five percent want to go to college but cannot, for any one of a number of reasons. All of the students want to succeed financially, and attending college is generally accepted as the first step toward that goal. The five percent who want to attend college but can't probably feel frustrated. They had the same goals as everyone else but were blocked from the usual means of achieving them. They may act out in a deviant manner.*

CHAPTER 6
DEVIANCE

Institutionalized Means to Success

In the 1960s, sociologists **Richard Cloward** and **Lloyd Ohlin** theorized that the most difficult task facing industrialized societies is finding and training people to take over the most intellectually demanding jobs from the previous generation. To progress, society needs a literate, highly trained work force. Society's job is to motivate its citizens to excel in the workplace, and the best way to do that is to foment discontent with the status quo. Cloward and Ohlin argued that if people were dissatisfied with what they had, what they earned, or where they lived, they would be motivated to work harder to improve their circumstances.

In order to compete in the world marketplace, a society must offer institutionalized means of succeeding. For example, societies that value higher education as a way to advance in the workplace must make educational opportunity available to everyone.

Illegitimate Opportunity Structures

Cloward and Ohlin further elaborated on Merton's strain theory. Deviant behavior—crime in particular—was not just a response to limited institutionalized means of success. Rather, crime also resulted from increased access to **illegitimate opportunity structures**, or various illegal means to achieve success. These structures, such as crime, are often more available to poor people living in urban slums. In the inner city, a poor person can become involved in prostitution, robbery, drug dealing, or loan sharking to make money. While these activities are clearly illegal, they often provide opportunities to make large amounts of money, as well as gain status among one's peers.

REACTIONS TO CULTURAL GOALS AND INSTITUTIONALIZED MEANS

Merton theorized about how members of a society respond to cultural goals and institutionalized means. He found that people adapt their goals in response to the means that society provides to achieve them. He identified five types of reactions:

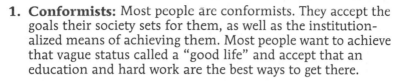

1. **Conformists:** Most people are conformists. They accept the goals their society sets for them, as well as the institution-alized means of achieving them. Most people want to achieve that vague status called a "good life" and accept that an education and hard work are the best ways to get there.

2. **Innovators:** These people accept society's goals but reject the usual ways of achieving them. Members of organized crime, who have money but achieve their wealth via deviant means, could be considered innovators.

3. **Ritualists:** A ritualist rejects cultural goals but still accepts the institutionalized means of achieving them. If a person who has held the same job for years has no desire for more money, responsibility, power, or status, he or she is a ritualist. This person engages in the same rituals every day but has given up hope that the efforts will yield the desired results.

4. **Retreatists:** Retreatists reject cultural goals as well as the institutionalized means of achieving them. They are not interested in making money or advancing in a particular career, and they tend not to care about hard work or about getting an education.

5. **Rebels:** Rebels not only reject culturally approved goals and the means of achieving them, but they replace them with their own goals. Revolutionaries are rebels in that they reject the status quo. If a revolutionary rejects capitalism or democracy, for example, he or she may attempt to replace it with his or her own form of government.

CHAPTER 6 DEVIANCE

Merton's Goals and Means

Method of adaptation	Cultural goals	Institutionalized means
Conformists	Accept	Accept
Innovators	Accept	Reject
Ritualists	Reject	Accept
Retreatists	Reject	Reject
Rebels	Reject/Replace	Reject/Replace

Conflict Perspective

A third important sociological framework is the conflict theory. Unlike the structural functional theory, which views society as a peaceful unit, **conflict theory** interprets society as a struggle for power between groups engaging in conflict for limited resources. **Karl Marx** is the founder of conflict theory. Conflict theorists like Marx posit that there are two general categories of people in industrialized societies: the capitalist class and the working class.

The **capitalist class**, or elite, consists of those in positions of wealth and power who own the means of production or control access to the means of production. The **working class** consists of relatively powerless individuals who sell their labor to the capitalist class. It is advantageous to the elite to keep the working class in a relatively disadvantaged position so that they can maintain the status quo and their own privileged positions.

CONFLICT THEORY AND CRIME

Conflict theorists believe that the broad division of people into these two categories is inherently unequal. They cite the criminal justice system to support their claim. The capitalist class passes laws designed to benefit themselves. These same laws are detrimental to the working class. Both groups commit acts of deviance, but the system the capitalists created defines deviance differently for each group. The criminal justice system judges and punishes each group differently.

In addition, the elite can often afford expensive lawyers and are sometimes on a first-name basis with the individuals in charge of making and enforcing laws. Members of the working class generally do not have these advantages.

White-Collar Crimes

Conflict theorists also look at the types of crimes committed by members of the two classes. The working class is more likely to commit so-called street crime, such as robbery, assault, or murder. Members of the elite are less likely to commit acts of violence but more likely to engage in **white-collar crime**, or nonviolent crime committed by the capitalist class during the course of their occupations.

> *EXAMPLE: White-collar criminal acts include embezzlement, insider stock trading, price fixing, and breaking regulatory laws.*

White-collar criminals are difficult to catch and prosecute for two main reasons:

- White-collar crime is difficult to identify. It leaves little physical evidence and no easily identifiable victim. In order to detect white-collar crime, authorities must have knowledge of high finance to discover that embezzlement, for example, has taken place.

- White-collar criminals are sometimes able to use their power and influence to avoid prosecution. Because of their social and economic clout, white-collar criminals rarely face criminal prosecution. When prosecuted, they are much less likely than members of the working class to receive a prison sentence. They are more likely to pay a fine as punishment for their crime.

White-Collar Crime: Not Dangerous? *Generally, white-collar crimes are not harmful or dangerous to the general public. But there are exceptions. In 2001, consumer advocates accused the Ford Motor Corporation of equipping some of their vehicles with faulty tires, made by Bridgestone/Firestone. Ford had already recalled the tires from vehicles sold in other countries but made no such recall on tires on those sold in the United States. Over 200 people died and more than 800 were injured in automobile accidents allegedly caused by the defective tires.*

CHAPTER 6
DEVIANCE

DEVIANCE AND POWER

Conflict theorist **Alexander Liazos** points out that the people we commonly label as deviant are also relatively powerless. According to Liazos, a homeless person living in the street is more likely to be labeled deviant than an executive who embezzles funds from the company he or she runs.

Because the people in positions of power make the laws of any given society, they create laws to benefit themselves. According to the conflict view of deviance, when rich and powerful people are accused of wrongdoing, they have the means to hire lawyers, accountants, and other people who can help them avoid being labeled as deviant. Lastly, members of a society generally believe that laws are inherently fair, which can draw attention away from the possibility that these laws might be unfairly applied or that a law itself might not be good or just.

Crime

White-collar crime is just one type of crime. **Crime**, or the violation of a written law, is a specific kind of deviance. What constitutes a crime varies from society to society.

In our society, sociologists have identified three general categories of crime:

1. **Crimes against the person:** These are crimes in which an act of violence is either threatened or perpetrated against a person. A mugging is an example of a crime against the person.

2. **Crimes against property:** These are crimes that involve the theft of property or certain forms of damage against the property of another. Arson is an example of a property crime.

3. **Victimless crimes:** These are crimes in which laws are violated, but there is no identifiable victim. Prostitution is often classified as a victimless crime.

PROFILE OF A CRIMINAL

Sociologists studying crime and deviance study statistics on who commits crime. Identifying a criminal profile can help sociologists understand the causes of crime and other deviance. Sociologists use the categories of age, gender, social class, and race and ethnicity to create this profile.

Age

Young people, roughly between the mid-teens and early twenties, commit almost 40 percent of all crimes. The likeliness to commit crime, particularly violent crime, decreases as one ages.

Gender

Men are arrested for crimes far more often than women. Men are arrested for approximately 70 percent of all property crimes and 80 percent of all violent crimes. Several theories, including the following, attempt to explain this situation:

- In all known societies, men are allowed more behavioral freedom than women are. More freedom means more opportunity to engage in deviant acts.

- Traditionally, police have been less willing to define a woman as a criminal, and the court system has been less likely to convict a woman and sentence her to jail or prison.

The gap between the number of arrests for men and the number of arrests for women is narrowing, however. This could be due to greater gender equality or, as some believe, to the rising number of women who commit crimes.

Social Class

Street crime, particularly violent crime, is more prevalent in poor, inner-city neighborhoods than in affluent communities. Violent crime in inner-city neighborhoods tends to be committed by the same group of seasoned criminals. Their victims are most often the law-abiding inhabitants of those neighborhoods. White-collar crime tends to occur in more affluent communities.

Race and Ethnicity

African Americans represent approximately 12 percent of the population in the United States and comprise 30 percent of property-crime arrests and 38 percent of violent-crime arrests. White people represent 66 percent of the arrests for property crimes and 60 percent of the arrests for violent crimes.

**CHAPTER 6
DEVIANCE**

According to crime statistics, African Americans, who
make up approximately 12 percent of the U.S. population,
compose 30 percent of the people arrested for property-
crime arrests and 38 percent of violent-crime arrests. Use
the symbolic interactionist, structural functionalist, and
conflict approaches from this chapter to analyze why
African Americans are more likely than other ethnic groups
to commit crime.

Are African Americans more prone to commit criminal acts or are
they simply overrepresented in crime statistics? The answer is a
complicated yes to both. Sociologists have many theories to
explain why African Americans commit more crime and are
arrested for more crime.

According to symbolic interactionists, African Americans are
more likely to commit crime because of the company they keep.
According to Sutherland, our family and friends play an important
role in how we act. Because a greater percentage of the African-
American community has committed a crime, blacks have more
opportunity than other groups to associate with released
criminals. These criminals may influence them to commit more
crime. The African-American population is also younger than
other populations. People under the age of twenty-five commit up
to 40 percent of all violent crime. Therefore, many blacks are of
the violent-crime-committing age.

A symbolic interactionist would also point to the powerful effect
of labeling. The public's perception of a person based on income
level, housing location, and appearance can affect attitudes toward
that person's actions. Society is more likely to label blacks as
criminals, regardless of any other factors. Once labeled as deviant,
African Americans are more likely to act in that manner. The
controversial law-enforcement technique of racial profiling is
based on labeling African Americans as deviant: Police officers
identify potential criminals based on skin color alone.

Student Essay

A structural functionalist would argue that African Americans commit more crime than whites because they are more often denied access to legitimate means of opportunity. Society commits fewer institutionalized means of support to African Americans. In 2003, blacks had the lowest median income of any ethnic group in the United States. Therefore, fewer African Americans are able to pursue educational opportunities that would allow them to earn more money and prestige. About 28 percent of all whites over the age of 25 have attended college. Only 17 percent of African Americans have, and of that group, two-thirds are women. Black men have one of the lowest college attendance rates of any population group in the United States.

A control theorist would argue that the criminal activity of African Americans is just another example of how the people in power—whites in particular—try to control blacks and define them as deviant. For example, whites create the laws and the punishments associated with them. They created stiffer laws and penalties for people caught using crack cocaine than using powder cocaine. African Americans are more likely to use crack; white Americans are more likely to use cocaine. White Americans caught using cocaine can often get out of serving jail time by agreeing to expensive detoxification programs. Poor African Americans cannot afford that option and are more likely to be sent to prison.

African Americans are not more likely to be deviant than other ethnic groups. Sociologists have shown that deviance is not a biological issue but rather a socially contested one.

Sample Test Questions

1. A teenager living in the inner city joins a gang and sells drugs. How would the social-interactionist sociologists Edwin Sutherland, Walter Reckless, and Howard Becker explain his deviance?

2. That teenager has been arrested for selling drugs. As his defense attorney, you have decided to bring in a sociologist to explain the teenager's behavior. Would you pick a symbolic interactionist, a structural functionalist, or a conflict theorist to defend your client? Explain your strategy.

3. Rosa Parks's act of deviance is noted as the launching point for the civil rights movement in the United States. What other historical acts of deviance later came to be known as heroic acts? What do these now-heroic acts suggest about the perception of deviance?

4. A lower-class Latino male steals $100 from a convenience store to pay for medicine his daughter needs. He is arrested and convicted to ten years in jail. A white male steals $100 million from his investors to pay for his luxurious homes and lavish parties. He is arrested but not convicted. How would sociologists explain this discrepancy?

5. Violent crime in the United States is down. Using what you learned in this chapter about crime, why do you think the crime rate has decreased?

6. John, a high school sophomore, occasionally drinks one beer. His friends don't care. His parents, however, are very upset and punish him severely. John responds by sneaking alcoholic beverages whenever he can. John's drinking illustrates
    - A. primary deviance
    - B. secondary deviance
    - C. positive sanction
    - D. outer control

7. *Which of the following is NOT one of the four elements of control that Travis Hirschi identified?*
   A. belief
   B. commitment
   C. involvement
   D. rebellion

8. *According to Robert Merton's strain theory, an educated person who stays in the same job without advancement for years is a*
   A. retreatist
   B. ritualist
   C. innovator
   D. conformist

9. *William Chambliss's study of teenage boys demonstrated the power of*
   A. labeling
   B. deviance
   C. negative sanctions
   D. crime

10. *Which contribution has conflict theory made to the understanding of deviance?*
   A. Deviance is behavior labeled deviant by society.
   B. If a society doesn't provide approved means to achieve specific goals, people will act out in a defiant manner.
   C. Deviance is defined by the people in control of society.
   D. People rely on their inner and outer controls to keep them from committing crime.

CHAPTER 6
DEVIANCE

ANSWERS

1. Symbolic interactionists offer several perspectives on why deviance occurs. According to Edwin Sutherland's theory of differential association, the teenager acts in a deviant manner because he learned how to from the people in his neighborhood and in his gang. His gang is a subversive subculture. Not all teenagers living in the inner city join gangs and sell drugs, however. According to Walter Reckless's theory of control, the teenager lacks some inner or outer control that would keep from him joining the gang or selling drugs. Becker might argue that selling drugs is deviant only because society has labeled it as outside its norms.

2. As defense attorney, I would choose a structural functionalist sociologist. He or she would focus on society's need for deviant behavior and its failure to provide the teenager with alternatives to criminal behavior. The witness would explain that the teenager's behavior, like all other deviance, is a necessary evil. In order for a society to clearly be able to define its norms and boundaries, it needs individuals who act outside those norms. The witness might also cite Merton, Cloward, and Ohlin, and argue that society failed to provide this teenager with the institutionalized means to success and thus forced him to pursue illegitimate opportunity structures.

3. Other deviant historical acts that became known as heroic include the Boston Tea Party, the American Revolution, and the hiding of Jews during the Holocaust. The Boston Tea Party and the American Revolution brought about the creation of our country. Families who hid Jews during the Holocaust risked the wrath of the German army to save thousands of people. The changed perception of these acts supports Howard Becker's theory of labeling. The acts were deviant at the time because they were labeled deviant. Today the acts are heroic because we label them as such.

4. Sociologists would point to the conflict theory to explain this situation. The white businessperson is part of the capitalist class. He not only helps to set the norms and laws of society but also has access to its powerful people. He can afford to hire the best lawyer to defend himself. He can use his resources to thwart the

government, which has more limited resources. The businessman committed a white-collar crime, which is generally more difficult to prove because of the difficulty involved in analyzing financial documents. The Latino male, on the other hand, is part of the working class. Unable to afford his daughter's medicine, he is unlikely to be able to afford a very good lawyer.

5. Violent crime is down in the United States because the American population is aging. Young people are most likely to commit violent crime, but their numbers are declining as an overall percentage of the population. Crime also goes down as the economy improves. During the 1990s, the U.S. economy boomed. It has been less stable since then, but overall the American standard of living has improved. Since poor people are more likely to commit crime, having fewer poor people would lead to less crime.

6. **B**

7. **D**

8. **B**

9. **A**

10. **C**

Summary

What Is Deviance?

- **Deviance** is any violation of society's norms.

- Each society defines deviance differently. Deviance is a relative issue and may differ based on **location, age, social status**, and **individual societies**.

- **Social control** is a way society has of encouraging conformity to norms. It consists of positive and negative sanctions.

- **Positive sanctions** are socially constructed expressions of approval.

- **Negative sanctions** are socially constructed expressions of disapproval.

Symbolic Interactionist Perspective

- The **symbolic interactionist perspective** is one of the main frameworks that sociologists use to analyze society. Symbolic interactionists view society as a byproduct of everyday social interaction.

- **Edwin Sutherland**'s **theory of differential association** asserts that deviance is a learned behavior that people learn from the different groups with which they associate. Some people form deviant subcultures based on a shared deviance.

- According to **William Reckless**'s **control theory**, people have two control systems to keep them from acting outside society's norms: inner and outer controls. **Inner controls** are internalized thought processes such as conscience. **Outer controls** include people who influence us.

- **Travis Hirschi** elaborated on control theory and identified four factors that make individuals more or less likely to commit deviance. These factors are **attachment, commitment, involvement**, and **belief**.

- **Howard Becker**'s **labeling theory** posits that deviant behavior is that which society labels as deviant.

- **Edwin Lemert** distinguished between **primary deviance**, the initial act, and **secondary deviance**, the repeated deviance that occurs in response to people's reaction to the primary deviance.

- **William Chambliss**'s study of boys he called the **Saints** and **Roughnecks** showed the power of labeling.

Structural Functional Theory

- Another sociological framework, the **structural functional theory**, focuses on society as a whole rather than the individuals within society.

- Deviance is a normal and necessary part of any society.

- **Émile Durkheim** said that deviance fulfills four functions for society: affirmation of cultural norms and values, clarification of right and wrong, unification of others in society, and bringing about social change.

- According to **Robert Merton**'s **strain theory** of deviance, when people are prevented from achieving culturally approved goals through institutionalized means, they experience strain that can lead to deviance.

- Denied access to **institutionalized means to success**, poor people turn to **illegitimate opportunity structures**.

- Merton identified five reactions to goals and institutionalized means: **conformists**, **innovators**, **ritualists**, **retreatists**, and **rebels**.

Conflict Perspective

- The **conflict theory** is **Karl Marx**'s theoretical paradigm that views society as struggle between groups over limited resources.

- Conflict theory identifies two categories of people in industrialized societies: the **capitalist class** and the **working class**. Those in positions of wealth and power make up the capitalist class. The working class sells its labor to the capitalist class.

**CHAPTER 6
DEVIANCE**

- The two classes are always in conflict with one another. Capitalists establish the norms of society; laws support them.

- Members of the capitalist class are less likely to be considered deviant because they make laws to benefit themselves.

- Members of the elite are more likely to commit **white-collar crime**, nonviolent crime committed in the course of their occupations.

- According to **Alexander Liazos**, people we commonly label as deviant are also relatively powerless.

Crime

- The three general categories of crime are **crimes against the person**, **crimes against property**, and **victimless crimes**.

- Age, gender, social class, and race and ethnicity are categories that sociologists use to create a criminal profile.

Social Stratification and Inequality

- Origins of Social Stratification
- Historical Stratification Systems
- Modern Stratification Systems
- Theories of Stratification
- Stratification System of the United States
- Social Classes in the United States
- Poverty in America
- Global Stratification

7

The United States is often described as a melting pot, a mass of people who have "melted" together and are essentially the same as one another. Some sociologists, however, prefer to think of America as a kaleidoscope, with a tremendous variety of people coming together to create a field of colors, rich with each individual's gender, race, religion, job, education, interests, and ethnic backgrounds.

This may sound like an idyllic, harmonious situation. But in the United States, as in societies around the world, people's differences not only result in a more diverse society but also lead to differences in the way they are treated, the opportunities available to them, how much money they earn, and the degree to which others respect them. These differences create layers, or *strata*, in society. How stratification occurs and the effects it has on people are major concerns of sociologists.

Origins of Social Stratification

In early societies, people shared a common social standing. As societies evolved and became more complex, they began to elevate some members. Today, **stratification**, a system by which society ranks its members in a hierarchy, is the norm throughout the world. All societies stratify their members. A **stratified** society is one in which there is an unequal distribution of society's rewards and in which people are arranged hierarchically into layers according to how much of society's rewards they possess. To understand stratification, we must first understand its origins.

HUNTING AND GATHERING SOCIETIES

Hunting and gathering societies had little stratification. Men hunted for meat while women gathered edible plants, and the general welfare of the society depended on all its members sharing what it had. The society as a whole undertook the rearing and socialization of children and shared food and other acquisitions more or less equally. Therefore, no group emerged as better off than the others.

HORTICULTURAL, PASTORAL, AND AGRICULTURAL SOCIETIES

The emergence of horticultural and pastoral societies led to social inequality. For the first time, groups had reliable sources of food: horticultural societies cultivated plants, while pastoral societies domesticated and bred animals. Societies grew larger, and not all members needed to be involved in the production of food. Pastoral societies began to produce more food than was needed for mere survival, which meant that people could choose to do things other than hunt for or grow food.

Division of Labor and Job Specialization

Division of labor in agricultural societies led to job specialization and stratification. People began to value certain jobs more highly than others. The further someone was from actual agriculture work, the more highly he or she was respected. Manual laborers became the least respected members of society, while those engaged in "high culture," such as art or music, became the most respected.

As basic survival needs were met, people began trading goods and services they could not provide for themselves and began accumulating possessions. Some accumulated more than others and gained prestige in society as a result. For some people, accumulating possessions became their primary goal. These individuals passed on what they had to future generations, concentrating wealth into the hands of a few groups.

INDUSTRIALIZED SOCIETIES

The Industrial Revolution began in Great Britain in the mid-1700s, when the steam engine came into use as a means of running other machines. The rise of industrialization led to increased social stratification. Factory owners hired workers who had migrated from rural areas in search of jobs and a better life. The owners exploited the workers to become wealthy, making them work long hours in unsafe conditions for very low wages. The gap between the "haves" and the "have-nots" widened.

The Improvement of Working Conditions

By the middle of the 1900s, workers had begun to secure rights for themselves, and the workplace became safer. Wages rose, and workers had something they had never had before: buying power. They could purchase homes, automobiles, and a vast array of consumer goods. Though their financial success was nothing compared to that of their bosses, the gap between the two was narrowing, and the middle class grew stronger.

CHAPTER 7
STRATIFICATION

At the same time, new forms of inequality took hold. The increasing sophistication and efficiency of factory machines led to the need for a different kind of worker—one who could not only operate certain kinds of equipment but could also read and write. The classification of the skilled worker was born. A **skilled worker** is literate and has experience and expertise in specific areas of production, or on specific kinds of machines. In contrast, many unskilled workers could neither read nor write English and had no specific training or expertise. The division arose between skilled and unskilled workers, with the former receiving higher wages and, as some would say, greater job security.

POSTINDUSTRIAL SOCIETIES

The rise of postindustrial societies, in which technology supports an information-based economy, has created further social stratification. Fewer people work in factories, while more work in service industries. Education has become a more significant determinant of social position. The Information Revolution has also increased global stratification. Even though new technology allows for a more global economy, it also separates more clearly those nations who have access to the new technology from those who don't.

Historical Stratification Systems

All societies are stratified, but the criteria used to categorize people vary widely. Social stratification has taken many forms throughout history, including slavery, the estate system, indentured servitude, the caste system, and the class system.

SLAVERY

Slavery is a system of stratification in which one person owns another, as he or she would own property, and exploits the slave's labor for economic gain. Slaves are one of the lowest categories in any stratification system, as they possess virtually no power or wealth of their own.

> **Slavery's Global History** *Many Americans view slavery as a phenomenon that began with the colonization of the New World and ended with the Civil War, but slavery has existed for a very long time. Slavery appears in the Old Testament of the Bible, as well as in the Qur'an. It was common practice in ancient Greece and Rome.*

The Causes of Slavery

A common assumption about slavery is that it is generally based on racism. Though racism was the primary cause of slavery in the United States, it was not the main reason that people in other areas were enslaved. Reasons for slavery include debt, crime, war, and beliefs of inherent superiority.

- **Debt:** Individuals who could not pay their way out of debt sometimes had to literally sell themselves. If a slave's debt was not paid off before his or her death, the debt was often passed down to his or her children, enslaving several generations of the same family.

- **Crime:** Families against whom a crime had been committed might enslave members of the perpetrator's family as compensation.

- **Prisoners of war:** Slaves were often taken during wartime, or when a new territory was being invaded. When Rome was colonizing much of the known world approximately 2,000 years ago, it routinely took slaves from the lands it conquered.

- **Beliefs of inherent superiority:** Some people believe that they have a right to enslave those who they believe are inherently inferior to them.

Slavery in the United States Slavery in the United States was unique for several reasons. First, it had a fairly equal male-to-female ratio. Slaves also lived longer than in other regions. They often reproduced, and their children were born into slavery. In other countries, slavery was not permanent or hereditary. Once slaves paid off their debts, they were set free. In the United States, slaves were rarely freed before the Civil War.

THE ESTATE SYSTEM

An ancient stratification system that no longer exists today was the **estate system**, a three-tiered system composed of the nobility, the clergy, and the commoners. During the Middle Ages, much of Europe was organized under this system.

Nobility

Members of the **nobility** had great inherited wealth and did little or no discernible work. They occupied themselves in what we would term leisure pursuits, such as hunting or riding. Others cultivated interests in cultural pursuits, such as art and music.

To ensure that their inherited wealth passed smoothly from one generation to the next without being dispersed to members of the extended family, the nobility of the Middle Ages practiced the law of primogeniture. The word **primogeniture** comes from Latin and means "first born." The nobility's law of primogeniture stipulated that only a first-born son could inherit his father's wealth. Members of this stratum developed an ideology to justify their privileged positions, the **divine right of kings**, which posited that the authority of the king comes directly from God. The king delegated authority to the nobles. Because the king and the nobles were God's representatives, they had to be obeyed.

Clergy

The eldest son was guaranteed a healthy income upon the death of his father, but other sons had to find their own means of income. Few, if any, were trained for work, so many became members of the Roman Catholic **clergy**, a body of religious officials. The clergy was very powerful in European society in the Middle Ages, and membership offered long-term job security and a comfortable living. The higher up the ladder a priest went, the more power he had over the masses.

Commoners

The third tier of the estate system consisted of the masses of people known as the **commoners**. They spent their lives engaged in hard physical labor, with virtually no chance of moving up in society.

INDENTURED SERVITUDE

Some commoners, searching for a way out of their situation, found it by agreeing to **indentured servitude**, in which one individual agrees to sell his or her body or labor to another for a specified period of time. Once the time period is over, the individual may leave. Indentured servitude differs from slavery in that the individual chooses to enter into the agreement, while slaves have no say in deciding the course of their lives.

Indentured servitude was a common practice for European commoners during the settlement of the American colonies. In the 1600s and 1700s, many people who wanted to come to America could not afford passage across the Atlantic Ocean. Instead, they entered into indentured servitude, selling their labor to the captain of an America-bound ship who, in turn, resold them to someone in America who needed workers. The terms of the contract lasted for an agreed-upon length of time, after which the new immigrant was free.

Modern Stratification Systems

In today's world, three main systems of stratification remain: slavery, a **caste system**, and a **class system**.

SLAVERY

Slavery still exists today. As many as 400 million people live under conditions that qualify as slavery, despite laws prohibiting it. In Mauritania, the Sudan, Ghana, and Benin, slavery exists much as it did 800 years ago. In other parts of the world, including Bangladesh, India, Nepal, and Pakistan, debt slavery is common. Sex slavery, the forcing of girls into prostitution, is prevalent in Asia.

CASTE SYSTEM

A **caste system** is a social system based on **ascribed statuses**, which are traits or characteristics that people possess as a result of their birth. Ascribed statuses can include race, gender, nationality, body type, and age. A caste system ranks people rigidly. No matter what a person does, he or she cannot change castes.

People often try to compensate for ascribed statuses by changing their nationality, lying about their age, or undergoing plastic surgery to alter their body type. In some societies, this strategy works; in others, it does not.

> EXAMPLE: *Religion is an ascribed status in some societies. Americans may convert to other religions, but in other countries, people may not change out of the particular religion into which they were born.*

India's Caste System

The Indian government officially outlawed the caste system in 1949, but vestiges of it remain today. The system originated with the Hindu religion, which subscribes to the concept of **reincarnation,** the belief that while the physical body dies, the soul of a person is immortal and goes on to be reborn into another body.

People who are good in their current life will come back to improved circumstances in the next life, but if they are evil, they will be punished in the next one. Therefore, those who are poor or ill are suffering punishment for having done something wrong in a past life. One should not interfere in the life of another person because that individual's circumstances are the result of what he or she has done in a previous incarnation.

Some might view reincarnation as religious tradition. Others might view it as **ideology**, a set of values that people devise to rationalize a particular social custom. In the case of the caste system, the custom being rationalized is inequality. If an individual is poor, for example, blaming his or her circumstances on what he or she did in a past life absolves others in the society of the responsibility for providing any assistance. Ideology also attempts to explain why some are in positions of wealth and power. Hindu tradition would say that the wealthy and powerful are being rewarded for what they did in a past life, and therefore they deserve every privilege they have.

The Five Castes

The Indian caste system has existed for about 3,000 years. There were four original castes, and one caste so low that it was not even considered to be part of the caste system:

1. The **Brahman** caste usually consisted of priests or scholars and enjoyed a great deal of prestige and wealth.

2. The **Kshatriya** caste, or warrior caste, was composed of those who distinguished themselves in military service.

3. The **Vaishva** caste comprised two sets of people—business-people and skilled craftspeople.

4. The **Shudra** caste consisted of those who made their living doing manual labor.

5. The **Harijan**, Dalit, or Untouchable caste was thought to comprise only inferior people who were so repulsive that an individual who accidentally touched one would have to engage in extensive ritual ablutions to rid himself or herself of the contamination.

There is no social movement in a caste system. An individual born into the Harijan caste cannot change his or her fate. Nor can someone be demoted to a lower caste; the caste into which a person is born is the caste he or she will have for life.

Castes and Work

Caste dictates the type of work an individual is allowed to do. Members of the Shudra caste, for example, are relegated to performing hard physical work regardless of their skill, intelligence, or ambition. Those born into the Brahman caste must attend university or become a member of the clergy, even though they may show no interest or aptitude toward that end.

Castes and Marriage

In a true caste system, societies practice **endogamy**, or marriage within one's own group or caste, with marriage between castes strictly forbidden. Traditionally, love is not used as a basis for marriage in a caste system. Rather, parents arrange marriages, sometimes when the future bride and groom are still children. The Indian concept of marriage is that while love is wonderful, it is neither a necessary nor desirable condition of marriage. If the couple is considered compatible in terms of major demographic variables, then the marriage is considered appropriate. Caste is one of the important variables, along with religion and educational level.

Modern India's caste system has many more than the original five castes. Because the distinctions between these numerous castes have blurred over time, some people marry outside their caste. In general, however, caste is still considered an important determinant of whom one will marry. When people do marry outside of their caste, they are likely to marry someone whose caste is only a few levels away from their own.

Castes and Socializing

One's caste also determines social contact. Friendships, and relationships in general, are rare among members of different castes. They neither live nor work near each other and rarely have any contact with one another.

> *South Africa's Apartheid System* The apartheid system of South Africa is another example of a caste system. The term **apartheid** refers to the total separation of the races. White Europeans colonized South Africa starting in the seventeenth century, and the area remained part of the British Empire until its independence in 1961. The policy of apartheid, introduced in 1948, relegated black people to a caste far below that of whites. Black people could not vote, receive an education, or mix with whites in any way. The work of Nelson Mandela and others who fought for black equality have made apartheid illegal in South Africa, but, like the caste system in India, some prejudice and discrimination remain.

CLASS SYSTEM

In a class system, an individual's place in the social system is based on **achieved statuses**, which are statuses that we either earn or choose and that are not subject to where or to whom we were born. Those born within a class system can choose their educational level, careers, and spouses. **Social mobility**, or movement up or down the social hierarchy, is a major characteristic of the class system.

The American Dream

The value referred to as the American Dream is indicative of the American social class system. The **American Dream** reflects what we see as the kind of equality of opportunity that can exist only in a class system. Americans believe that all people, regardless of the conditions into which they were born, have an equal chance to achieve success.

Part of the American Dream is the belief that every child can grow up to be president of the United States. Former president Bill Clinton, for example, came from a relatively poor background and grew up in a small town in Arkansas. His father died before he was born, and he was raised by his mother and abusive stepfather. Clinton rose above his humble beginnings to attend prestigious universities, receive a Rhodes Scholarship, and enjoy a successful career in politics that began with his election as governor of Arkansas.

Theories of Stratification

For centuries, sociologists have analyzed social stratification, its root causes, and its effects on society. Theorists Karl Marx and Max Weber disagreed about the nature of class, in particular. Other sociologists applied traditional frameworks to stratification.

KARL MARX

Karl Marx based his conflict theory on the idea that modern society has only two classes of people: the bourgeoisie and the proletariat. The **bourgeoisie** are the owners of the means of production: the factories, businesses, and equipment needed to produce wealth. The **proletariat** are the workers.

According to Marx, the bourgeoisie in capitalist societies exploit workers. The owners pay them enough to afford food and a place to live, and the workers, who do not realize they are being exploited, have a false consciousness, or a mistaken sense, that they are well off. They think they can count on their capitalist bosses to do what was best for them.

Marx foresaw a workers' revolution. As the rich grew richer, Marx hypothesized that workers would develop a true class consciousness, or a sense of shared identity based on their common experience of exploitation by the bourgeoisie. The workers would unite and rise up in a global revolution. Once the dust settled after the revolution, the workers would then own the means of production, and the world would become communist. No one stratum would control the access to wealth. Everything would be owned equally by everyone.

Marx's vision did not come true. As societies modernized and grew larger, the working classes became more educated, acquiring specific job skills and achieving the kind of financial well-being that Marx never thought possible. Instead of increased exploitation, they came under the protection of unions and labor laws. Skilled factory workers and tradespeople eventually began to earn salaries that were similar to, or in some instances greater than, their middle-class counterparts.

MAX WEBER

Max Weber took issue with Marx's seemingly simplistic view of stratification. Weber argued that owning property, such as factories or equipment, is only part of what determines a person's social class. Social class for Weber included power and prestige, in addition to property or wealth. People who run corporations without owning them still benefit from increased production and greater profits.

Prestige and Property

Weber argued that property can bring prestige, since people tend to hold rich people in high regard. Prestige can also come from other sources, such as athletic or intellectual ability. In those instances, prestige can lead to property, if people are willing to pay for access to prestige. For Weber, wealth and prestige are intertwined.

Power and Wealth

Weber believed that social class is also a result of power, which is merely the ability of an individual to get his or her way, despite opposition. Wealthy people tend to be more powerful than poor people, and power can come from an individual's prestige.

> **EXAMPLE:** *Arnold Schwarzenegger enjoyed prestige as a bodybuilder and as an actor, and he was also enormously wealthy. When he was elected governor of California in 2004, he became powerful as well.*

Sociologists still consider social class to be a grouping of people with similar levels of wealth, prestige, and power.

DAVIS AND MOORE: THE FUNCTIONALIST PERSPECTIVE

Sociologists **Kingsley Davis** and **Wilbert Moore** believed that stratification serves an important function in society. In any society, a number of tasks must be accomplished. Some tasks, such as cleaning streets or serving coffee in a restaurant, are relatively simple. Other tasks, such as performing brain surgery or designing skyscrapers, are complicated and require more intelligence

CHAPTER 7
STRATIFICATION

and training than the simple tasks. Those who perform the difficult tasks are therefore entitled to more power, prestige, and money. Davis and Moore believed that an unequal distribution of society's rewards is necessary to encourage people to take on the more complicated and important work that required many years of training. They believed that the rewards attached to a particular job reflect its importance to society.

MELVIN TUMIN

Sociologist **Melvin Tumin** took issue with Davis and Moore's theory. He disagreed with their assumption that the relative importance of a particular job can always be measured by how much money or prestige is given to the people who performed those jobs. That assumption made identifying important jobs difficult. Were the jobs inherently important, or were they important because people received great rewards to perform them?

If society worked the way Davis and Moore had envisioned, Tumin argued, all societies would be **meritocracies**, systems of stratification in which positions are given according to individual merit. Ability would determine who goes to college and what jobs someone holds. Instead, Tumin found that gender and the income of an individual's family were more important predictors than ability or what type of work an individual would do. Men are typically placed in a higher social stratification than women, regardless of ability. A family with more money can afford to send its children to college. As college graduates, these children are more likely to assume high-paying, prestigious jobs. Conversely, people born into poverty are more likely to drop out of school and work low-paying jobs in order to survive, thereby shutting them off from the kinds of positions that are associated with wealth, power, and prestige.

The Stratification System of the United States

Like all societies, the United States is stratified, and this stratification is often based on a person's **socioeconomic status (SES)**. This complex formula takes into account three factors:

- Education
- Occupation
- Income

The number of years a person spends in school, plus the prestige of his or her occupation, plus the amount of money he or she makes, determine one's social class. While this method of dividing up the population into classes might be useful, it has several shortcomings.

EDUCATION

One determinant of socioeconomic status is education. People with a high school degree are classified in one group. People with college degrees are put into another. Using educational attainment levels to indicate SES is problematic for two reasons:

- School systems in this country are not uniform in quality.
- Not everyone has equal access to primary, secondary, and higher education.

Free, compulsory education has existed in the United States since the beginning of the twentieth century, but some school systems are better than others. The American public education system tends to be highly decentralized, with decisions about what to include in the school curriculum being made at the state or local level. School systems differ widely in what they choose to teach and when.

Disparity of Resources Among Public Schools

Some school systems produce graduates who are prepared for higher education, while others turn out people whose basic math and language skills are so poor that they qualify for only a few types of jobs. The quality of the education a school provides depends largely on its budget, which in turn relies heavily on the tax base of the town or city in which it is located. Wealthy cities can afford better teachers, newer materials, and superior technology, whereas poor cities can barely afford basic supplies.

Poorer communities also tend to have a higher dropout rate than wealthier communities. Therefore, while establishing a profile of a typical high school graduate is difficult, the assumption remains, for the purposes of social classification, that all high school graduates are equally prepared for either the workplace or for higher education.

Disparity in Higher Education

The reliance on educational level as an indicator of social class becomes more problematic when one considers the huge variety of colleges in the United States. There are vocational schools, junior colleges, four-year colleges, and universities. Some colleges prepare individuals for specific careers, whereas others emphasize the development of intellectual and life skills. Religiously oriented colleges focus on development of the spirit and the teaching of theology as well as academic material. Some colleges encourage their students to pursue graduate degrees, whereas others assist middle-aged people in returning to college after long absences from the academic sphere.

Cost of Higher Education

As the quality of higher education varies, so does the cost of attending college. Even if our federal government completely subsidized the cost of a college education, as governments in some countries do, the financial circumstances of some individuals would preclude them from seeking higher education.

OCCUPATION

Occupational prestige is very subjective and varies from country to country. In the United States, as in most industrialized societies, jobs requiring extensive schooling and intellectual acuity, and that afford the greatest degrees of professional autonomy, are considered the most prestigious. These occupations include:

- Physicians
- Judges
- University professors
- CEOs

Jobs requiring manual labor, or in which a person serves or cleans up after others, tend to be low-prestige occupations:

- Mechanic
- Truck driver
- Maid
- Janitor

Prestigious jobs are not always the easiest jobs to hold. The occupation of physician is very prestigious but requires a long and expensive education, very long hours, and unpredictable lawsuits from litigious patients. Electricians also spend years in specialized training before they can become licensed. Electricians generally have reliable, steady income. They don't have to work the 24-hour shifts that doctors do. Unionized electricians have additional job security and receive benefits that physicians in private practice must provide for themselves. Still, physicians enjoy a higher prestige.

Despite the cautions detailed below, occupation tells us the most about a person. Knowing what somebody does for a living gives us an approximate idea of the extent of his or her education and provides us with a very rough estimate of how much money he or she makes.

STRATIFICATION
CHAPTER 7

Work Preference

Using one's occupation as a partial measure of social class has another pitfall: it assumes that people are doing the kinds of work they prefer and for which they are best prepared. In a full market employment economy, people can generally find the kinds of work they want, but in a weak economy, people sometimes have to take jobs that do not reflect their interests, education, or experience.

Bias

Using occupation to place people in a certain social class reflects our society's bias. As mentioned earlier, American society automatically accords some jobs more prestige than others. This does not mean that they are better occupations or that the people who do them are more worthy individuals.

INCOME

Of the three variables, income is perhaps the least reliable as a predictor of SES. Assuming that a person's income is derived mostly from his or her job, the salary he or she receives is subject to influence by a variety of factors:

- Geographic region
- Size of company
- Educational level
- Work experience

> **EXAMPLE:** *Being vice president of a company could mean many different things. In a small company in the rural South, the vice president of a company might make $30,000 a year, whereas the vice president of a Fortune 500 company would very likely have a six-figure salary. In the banking industry, vice president is a common term. It's often given to people who make a certain salary, regardless of their actual position or level of responsibility.*

Social Classes in the United States

Socioeconomic status is just a way of describing the stratification system of the United States. The class system, also imperfect in classifying all Americans, nonetheless offers a general understanding of American social stratification. The United States has roughly six social classes:

1. Upper class
2. New money
3. Middle class
4. Working class
5. Working poor
6. Poverty level

THE UPPER CLASS OR OLD MONEY

The **upper class**, which makes up about one percent of the U.S. population, generally consists of those with vast inherited wealth (sometimes called "old money"). Members of the upper class may also have a recognizable family name, such as Rockefeller, DuPont, or Kennedy. Some members of the upper class work, but their salaries are not their primary sources of income. Most members of this strata have attended college, most likely at some of the most prestigious educational institutions in the country.

> EXAMPLE: *The Kennedy family is a prime example of an upper-class family. Joseph P. Kennedy made his fortune during the 1920s and passed it down to succeeding generations.*

NEW MONEY

The category called **new money** is a relatively new rung on the social ladder and makes up about 15 percent of the population. New money includes people whose wealth has been around only for a generation or two. Also referred to as the *nouveaux riches* (French for "newly rich"), they have earned their money rather than inheriting it. Unlike the members of the upper class, they do not have a family associated with old money.

> *EXAMPLE: Oprah Winfrey, Michael Jordan, Bill Gates, and other celebrities, athletes, and business people fit into this category.*

The *nouveaux riches* merit their own category because they make so much money that they lead very different lives from those in subsequent SES groupings. The newly rich simply do not have the day-to-day financial concerns that often plague the rest of society.

THE MIDDLE CLASS

The next rung on the ladder is the **middle class**, which includes about 34 percent of the population. The members of the middle class earn their money by working at what could be called professional jobs. They probably have college educations, or at least have attended college. These people are managers, doctors, lawyers, professors, and teachers. They rarely wear uniforms, although some might wear distinctive clothing, such as a physician's white coat. They are often referred to as the **white-collar** class, referring to the tendency of many middle-class men to wear suits with a white shirt to work.

THE WORKING CLASS

The **working class** makes up about 30 percent of the population. Its members may have gone to college, but more have had vocational or technical training. The members of the working class have a variety of jobs, including the following:

- Electrician
- Carpenter
- Factory worker
- Truck driver
- Police officer

This category is also called the **blue-collar** class in recognition of the likelihood that many of these individuals wear uniforms to work rather than suits. People in the working class are more likely to be members of unions than are people in the middle class. While there are differences between the working class and the middle class in terms of their values, behaviors, and even their voting records, their standards of living are often similar, but not identical.

THE WORKING POOR

Another new rung on the socioeconomic ladder is the **working poor**. Estimating how many Americans are in this category is difficult because the line separating them from those who are at or below the poverty level (see next section) is not solid. Estimates say that approximately 20 percent of the population could be classified in either the working-poor or poverty-level categories.

People in the working-poor category have a low educational level, are not highly skilled, and work at minimum-wage jobs. They often work two or more part-time jobs and receive no health insurance or other benefits. These individuals are vulnerable to falling below the poverty line. They have very little or no job security, and their jobs are easily outsourced to countries where labor is cheaper.

Every economy needs a group of workers that it can hire during an economic upswing and lay off when the economy weakens. The members of the working poor are such people; they are the "last hired, first fired."

THE POVERTY LEVEL

People at the **poverty level** lack the means to meet their basic needs for food, clothing, and shelter. The poverty level, set by the federal government in the mid 1960s, is an estimate of the minimum income a family of four needs to survive. The poverty level is currently about $18,000 per year—a figure that has come under fire for being woefully inadequate, mainly because poor people, particularly those in urban areas with high costs of living, need more money to survive.

CHAPTER 7
STRATIFICATION

Poverty in America

A staggering number of Americans currently live below the poverty level. In order to solve the problem of the nation's poor, we must first understand who and where they are.

WHO ARE POOR PEOPLE?

About 66 percent of poor people are white, reflecting the fact that white people outnumber people of other races and ethnic groups in the United States. About 25 percent of the people living in poverty are black. The term **feminization of poverty** refers to the increasing number of female-headed households living at or below the poverty level. In the 1960s, approximately 25 percent of all female-headed households were in poverty; that figure is about 50 percent today. An increasing number of children are affected by this trend. As of 2005, about 16 percent of children under age 18 live in poverty; about 80 percent of them live in households headed by a single female.

WHERE ARE POOR PEOPLE?

Though all states have poverty, poor people are concentrated in the inner cities and in the rural South. Social economist **William Julius Wilson** believes that the relatively high level of poverty in inner cities is due to the lack of jobs. He says that many companies have relocated to suburban areas or have downsized their urban operations. Still others have moved their manufacturing facilities to other countries to take advantage of cheaper labor costs and laws favoring the development of new businesses.

The rural South has a high rate of poverty for several reasons:

- Manufacturing concerns have preferred to operate in suburban areas, which are closer to interstate highways, railroads, and airports that enable manufacturers to transport their products.

- Educational levels in the South tend to be lower. About 12 percent of the general U.S. population drops out of high school; in the South the dropout rate is about 15 percent.

- The increasing demands of technology require employees who are flexible, skilled, and able to learn rapidly. A workforce composed of people with relatively low levels of education and few job skills is simply not attractive to potential employers.

THE CONSEQUENCES OF POVERTY

More than any other social class, the poor suffer from short life expectancies and health problems, including heart disease, high blood pressure, and mental illness. Reasons include the following:

- Poor people are often not well educated about diet and exercise. They are more likely than people in higher social strata to be overweight and suffer from nutritional deficits.

- They are less likely to have health insurance, so they put off going to the doctor until a problem seems like a matter of life and death. At that time they must find a public health facility that accepts patients with little or no insurance.

- Living in poverty brings chronic stress. Poor people live every day with the uncertainty of whether they can afford to eat, pay the electric bill, or make the rent payment. Members of the middle class also have stress but have more options for addressing it.

- Poor people usually do not have jobs that offer them vacation time to let them relax.

- High levels of unresolved stress, financial problems, and poor health can wreak havoc within a relationship. Poor people report more relationship problems than do people in other classes and have higher rates of divorce and desertion. The children of such families are more likely than their middle-class counterparts to grow up in broken homes or in single-parent, female-headed households.

CHAPTER 7 STRATIFICATION

THE CULTURE OF POVERTY

Anthropologist **Oscar Lewis** coined the term **culture of poverty**, which means that poor people do not learn the norms and values that can help them improve their circumstances; hence, they become trapped in a repeated pattern of poverty. Because many poor people live in a narrow world in which all they see is poverty and desperation, they never acquire the skills or the ambition that could help them rise above the poverty level. Since culture is passed down from one generation to the next, parents teach their children to accept their circumstances rather than to work to change them. The cycle of poverty then becomes self-perpetuating.

Though the stratification system of the United States is based on class rather than on caste, some people claim that a racial caste system exists in this country. Slavery was outlawed after the Civil War, but some believe it was replaced by another prejudicial system—a caste system based on race. Though whites could no longer own slaves, they still considered themselves to be superior to people of African descent. They insisted on separate recreational, educational, and other facilities for themselves and their families and even prevented intermarriage between people of different races. Before this time, one's race was a strong indicator of destiny, and some would say that there is still a racial caste system in the United States today.

Global Stratification

Not only is each society stratified, but in a global perspective, societies are stratified in relation to one another. Sociologists employ three broad categories to denote global stratification: most industrialized nations, industrializing nations, and least industrialized nations. In each category, countries differ on a variety of factors, but they also have differing amounts of the three basic components of the American stratification system: wealth (as defined by land and money), power, and prestige.

The countries that could be considered the **most industrialized** include the United States, Canada, Japan, Great Britain, France, and the other industrialized countries of Western Europe, all of which are capitalistic. **Industrializing nations** include most of the countries of the former Soviet Union. The **least industrialized nations** account for about half of the land on Earth and include almost 70 percent of the world's people. These countries are primarily agricultural and tend to be characterized by extreme poverty. The majority of the residents of the least industrialized nations do not own the land they farm, and many lack running water, indoor plumbing, and access to medical care. Their life expectancy is low when compared to residents of richer countries, and their rates of illness are higher.

THEORIES OF GLOBAL STRATIFICATION

Several theories purport to explain how the world became so highly stratified.

Colonialism

Colonialism exists when a powerful country invades a weaker country in order to exploit its resources, thereby making it a colony. Those countries that were among the first to industrialize, such as Great Britain, were able to make colonies out of a number of foreign countries. At one time, the British Empire included India, Australia, South Africa, and countries in the Caribbean, among others. France likewise colonized many countries in Africa, which is why in countries such as Algeria, Morocco, and Mali French is spoken in addition to the countries' indigenous languages.

World System Theory

Immanuel Wallerstein's **world system theory** posited that as societies industrialized, capitalism became the dominant economic system, leading to the globalization of capitalism. The **globalization of capitalism** refers to the adoption of capitalism by countries around the world. Wallerstein said that as capitalism spread, countries around the world became closely interconnected. For example, seemingly remote events that occur on the other side of the world can have a profound impact on daily life in the United States. If a terrorist attack on a Middle Eastern oil pipeline interrupts production, American drivers wind up paying more for fuel because the cost of oil has risen.

Neocolonialism

Sociologist **Michael Harrington** used the term **neocolonialism** to describe the tendency of the most industrialized nations to exploit less-developed countries politically and economically. Powerful countries sell goods to less-developed countries, allowing them to run up enormous debts that take years to pay off. In so doing, the most developed nations gain a political and economic advantage over the countries that owe them money.

Multinational Corporations

Sometimes, **multinational corporations**, large corporations that do business in a number of different countries, can exploit weak or poor countries by scouring the globe for inexpensive labor and cheap raw materials. These corporations often pay a fraction of what they would pay for the same goods and employees in their home countries. Though they do contribute to the economies of other countries, the real beneficiaries of their profits are their home countries. Multinational corporations help to keep the global stratification system in place.

Do you think that differences in education, occupation, and income adequately explain the stratification system in the United States? Or are there other factors that play a significant role?

American society is stratified by a person's education level, choice of work, and income. Of these three criteria, income is the most important to Americans. These categories are not sufficient, however, in clearly explaining the different social groups in the United States. Gender, race, and ethnicity complicate these distinctions.

Gender affects the educational, occupational, and money-earning opportunities for women and creates a substratum within each socioeconomic group. Even if women receive the same education, choose the same occupational field, and start with the same salary as men, they are still likely to earn less money than men over the course of their lives. The main reason that the average woman makes 76 cents to every dollar a man makes is that women are more likely to take time off to care for children. Once a woman curtails her career to care for her children, she is unable to catch up to a man who did not stop his career.

Women who stay at home with their children are another substratum. They work without earning a salary, and their occupation affords them little prestige or power. Yet some stay-at-home mothers enjoy an elevated social status because of their husbands' income or occupation. The simplistic view that stratification is dependent on education, income, and occupation gets more complicated when gender is added into the mix.

Race and ethnicity also influence social stratification. Many people believe that a racial caste system, based on the legacy of slavery and discrimination, still exists in the United States. As for women, ethnic minorities of either gender can share the same educational pedigree as white people, yet we wouldn't necessarily put them in the same social class. Race and ethnicity also influence and sometimes limit occupational opportunities.

Student Essay

Affirmative action has helped to open up more opportunities, but young African Americans and those from other ethnic groups have fewer successful role models to emulate. Without role models and mentors, minorities may not be successful when reaching for an occupation different than that of their parents or grandparents.

Gender, race, and ethnicity are important dimensions to understanding stratification in the United States. They complicate the simple categories of education, income, and occupation and offer a more complete picture of how American society is layered.

Sample Test Questions

1. Compare and contrast the estate system and the caste system.

2. How does disparity in public schools contribute to the culture of poverty in the United States?

3. Is the American Dream available to all people? Why or why not?

4. Is it easier to attain wealth when you have prestige or to attain prestige when you have wealth?

5. How can you explain the feminization of poverty?

6. Which of the following is NOT a cause of slavery?
   A. debt
   B. crime
   C. war
   D. stratification

7. Marx and Weber disagreed on the importance of _____ in determining class.
   A. power
   B. prestige
   C. wealth
   D. conflict

8. What is the key distinction between a caste system and a class system?
   A. social mobility
   B. educational opportunity
   C. occupational prestige
   D. endogamy

9. *Which of the following is NOT a consequence of poverty?*
   A.   Poor people are more likely to be overweight and have nutritional difficulties.
   B.   Poor people are more likely to have health insurance.
   C.   Poor people have a lower life expectancy.
   D.   Poor people have higher rates of divorce and desertion.

10. *How do colonialism and neocolonialism contribute to world stratification?*
   A.   by allowing a more powerful country to dominate a less developed nation
   B.   by allowing powerful nations to send their lower classes to other countries
   C.   by reviving the estate system
   D.   by reviving the caste system

CHAPTER 7
STRATIFICATION

ANSWERS

1. Both systems stratify society based on ascribed status, although the estate system is a bit more flexible. Both systems use religious or spiritual ideology to justify stratification. Both dictate occupation, marriage, and relationship options. In the estate system, the nobles are born into that class. They claim their authority through the divine right of kings. Members of the clergy are born into nobility and then become priests, while commoners rarely move out of their position. Unlike the caste system, the estate system no longer exists. The caste system, though no longer legal, still exists in places such as India. Hindus based the caste system on the religious ideology of reincarnation. Indians cannot change castes.

2. Education remains an important avenue to success in the United States. Without quality education, poor children are unlikely to learn how to rise out of poverty. Schools in poor areas lack the resources to train students adequately, and the students do not learn enough in high school to be accepted into college. Even if they do aspire to attend college, they may not learn how to navigate the college-application process, since poor schools often lack counselors dedicated to helping students get into college. Students who don't attend college generally work at lower-paying jobs and can't afford to leave poor areas. As a result, their kids will attend the same school they did, and the cycle of poverty will continue.

3. Theoretically, the American Dream is available to all people living in the United States—native-born Americans as well as immigrants. However, the dream is easier for some to attain than others. White people, particularly men, have the easiest time attaining the American Dream. White men have more institutional support for their ambitions, and society expects more from them than from others. They are more likely to receive help from people who want them to succeed. For women and minorities, policies such as affirmative action and anti-discrimination legislation are in place to help them succeed. Policies cannot, however, overcome all resistance. For women, glass ceilings prevent them from reaching the highest echelons of business, and racism and a racist caste system often prevent ethnic minorities from reaching their potential. Still, women

and minorities have achieved success in many areas of American life. If it's possible for some, it is possible for others—even if some people face greater difficulties.

4. In the United States, money begets prestige and power. It is easier to attain prestige when you have wealth. Americans often have greater respect for a person who is very wealthy than for someone who is a great humanitarian but has little money. Prestige does not always correlate with wealth, however. Some people gain prestige as a result of their professions, not as a result of the salary they receive. Supreme Court justices receive salaries of less than $200,000 a year but are esteemed members of society. Third-string players in the NBA receive higher salaries than the justices but probably have less prestige. In another example, a lottery winner can be a person of average intelligence and charisma, but when he becomes wealthy, he gains prestige.

5. Several factors have combined to explain the increased number of women and children living at or below the poverty level in the United States. First, more women are choosing to live alone, whereas in the past, such a choice was considered deviant. Women in abusive situations used to have few choices other than staying in the abusive relationship. Today, however, single motherhood is no longer considered deviant, so more women opt for it if they are in an abusive relationship. Divorce for reasons other than abuse is also more common today. After a divorce, a woman's standard of living is likely to decline, since women still only make about three-quarters of what men make.

6. **D**

7. **C**

8. **A**

9. **B**

10. **A**

CHAPTER 7
STRATIFICATION

Summary

The Origins of Social Stratification

- All modern societies are **stratified**, arranged hierarchically into layers due to an unequal distribution of society's rewards.

- Hunting and gathering societies had no social stratification because all members had to produce food and share it.

- Stratification arose with **job specialization** that began in pastoral and horticulture societies. Not everyone in the society needed to be involved in food production.

- Rise of industrialized societies led to increased stratification as the difference between the haves and the have-nots grew.

- Some improvement in working conditions created a **middle class**.

- New technologies created a new social group, **skilled workers**.

- The new technology used in postindustrial societies contributed to increased worldwide stratification.

Historical Stratification Categories

- Historical stratification systems include **slavery, the estate system**, and **indentured servitude**.

- **Slavery** is a system of stratification in which one person owns another.

- The **estate system**, prevalent in the Middle Ages, was a three-tiered system composed of the **nobility**, **clergy**, and **commoners**.

- Some commoners sought new opportunities in the New World and agreed to **indentured servitude** to get there. Unlike slavery, in which the enslaved have no choice, indentured servants agree to sell their bodies or labor to someone for a specified period of time.

Modern Stratification Systems

- Slavery still exists as a stratification system.

- The **caste** system is based on **ascribed status**, which is a condition of birth, and allows little or no possibility for mobility.

- India's caste system is based on a belief in **reincarnation**, the belief that while the physical body dies, the soul of a person is immortal and goes on to be reborn into another body.

- People in castes must marry within their own caste. This practice is known as **endogamy**.

- **Social mobility** is an important characteristic of the **class** system, which is based on **achieved status**.

- The United States has a class system of stratification.

Theories of Stratification

- **Karl Marx** argued that there were only two classes of people in any capitalist society: the **bourgeoisie** and the **proletariat**. He believed that the proletariat would eventually realize they were being exploited by the bourgeoisie and would rise up in revolution.

- **Max Weber** argued that owning property was only part of determining a person's social class. **Power** and **prestige** were equally important.

- **Kingsley Davis** and **Wilbert Moore** believed that stratification served an important function for society. It provided greater rewards to people willing to take more complex jobs.

- **Melvin Tumin** disagreed, arguing that all societies are not **meritocracies**, systems of stratification in which positions are given according to individual merit. **Gender** and a family's **wealth** contribute to social class.

CHAPTER 7
STRATIFICATION

The Stratification System of the United States

- A person's **socioeconomic status (SES)** is based on **education, occupation,** and **income**.

- These categories are not always reliable predictors of social class.

Social Classes in the United States

- Sociologists have identified six social classes in the United States.

- The **upper class,** which makes up about one percent of the U.S. population, generally consists of those with vast inherited wealth (sometimes called "old money").

- The category called **new money** includes rich people whose wealth is relatively new. This class makes up about 15 percent of the population.

- The **middle class,** about 34 percent of the population, includes people who work at professional or **white-collar** jobs.

- Members of the **working class,** about 30 percent of the population, often work at **blue-collar** jobs.

- The **working poor** are people who have little to no job security and who, despite working two or more jobs, barely earn enough money to survive.

- People at the **poverty level** lack the means to meet their basic needs for food, clothing, and shelter.

Poverty in America

- A staggering number of Americans currently live below the poverty level.

- Many people living in poverty are women. The **feminization of poverty** refers to the increasing number of female-headed households living at or below the poverty level.

- **William Julius Wilson** found that poverty is concentrated in inner cities and the rural South.

- Poverty exacts a high emotional and physical toll on individuals.

- According to **Oscar Lewis**, poor people do not learn the norms and values that can help them improve their circumstances, hence they get trapped in a **culture of poverty**.

Global Stratification

- Societies are stratified in relation to one another.

- The three broad categories of global stratification are **most-industrialized nations**, **industrializing nations**, and **least-industrialized nations**.

- Each category differs in wealth, power, and prestige.

- Theories of global stratification include **colonialism**, **world system theory**, **neocolonialism**, and **multinational corporations**.

- **Colonialism** occurs when a powerful country invades a weaker country in order to exploit its resources.

- According to **Wallerstein**'s **world system theory**, as societies industrialized, capitalism became the dominant economic system, which led to the **globalization of capitalism**.

- **Harrington**'s theory of **neocolonialism** argues that most industrialized nations tend to politically and economically exploit less developed countries.

- **Multinational corporations** help maintain the global stratification system.

CHAPTER 7 STRATIFICATION

Major Figures

Note from SparkNotes: Not all of the people mentioned in the text are listed here. We've narrowed the list to include only those figures you're most likely to be tested on.

Asch, Solomon (1907–1996) A psychologist who investigated social conformity by studying how people reacted when their perceptions of events were challenged by others. Asch found that most individuals changed their own opinions in order to agree with the group, even when the majority was clearly wrong.

Becker, Howard (1899–1960) The sociologist who developed the labeling theory of deviance. Becker concluded that the labels a person is assigned in society dictate his or her behavior.

Chambliss, William (1933–) The sociologist who performed the "Saints and Roughnecks" study. Chambliss discovered the extent to which the labels attached to two groups of individuals during high school affected their success later in life.

Cloward, Richard (1926–2001) and Lloyd Ohlin (1918–) Sociologists who theorized that the greatest responsibility of industrialized societies was to prepare the next generation of workers. Cloward and Ohlin also developed the concept of "illegitimate opportunity structure," or access to various illegal means for achieving success.

Cooley, Charles Horton (1864–1929) A sociologist whose theory of socialization was called the "looking-glass self." Cooley said that we develop our self-images through our interactions with significant others. He referred to "significant others" as those people in our lives whose opinions matter to us and who are in a position to influence the way we think about things, especially about ourselves.

Davis, Kingsley (1908–1997) and Wilbert Moore (1914–1988) Sociologists who believed that stratification served an important function in society. Davis and Moore theorized that an unequal distribution of society's rewards was necessary to encourage people to take on complicated work that required many years of training.

Du Bois, W. E. B. (1868–1963) A pioneering theorist on African-American subculture, a civil rights activist, and author of the groundbreaking 1903 masterpiece of sociology and literature *The Souls of Black Folk*. Du Bois examined in detail the economic and social conditions of African Americans in the three decades that followed the Civil War.

Durkheim, Émile (1858–1917) A French sociologist who explored links between social integration and suicide rates. Durkheim hypothesized that members of groups that lacked a high degree of social integration were more likely to commit suicide. He also believed that deviance is a natural and necessary part of any society and listed four ways in which deviants serve society.

Freud, Sigmund (1856–1939) The father of psychoanalysis, or the analysis of the mind. Freud was interested in how the mind developed and said that the healthy adult mind consists of three parts: the id, superego, and ego.

Garfinkel, Harold (1917–) The sociologist responsible for the theory of ethnomethodology (1967). Garfinkel also coined the term *degradation ceremony* to describe how an individual's identity can be negatively affected when his or her deviance becomes known to others.

Gilligan, Carol (1933–) An educational psychologist who analyzes the link between gender and social behavior. Her early work focused on exposing the gender biases in Lawrence Kohlberg's studies of moral development. Boys focus on rules and justice, whereas girls are more likely to consider relationships and feelings.

Goffman, Erving (1922–1982) The developer of the theory of dramaturgy and the concepts of stigma, spoiled identity, and impression management, among others. Goffman believed that we are all actors playing roles on the stage of everyday life. He also developed the concept of a total institution, which is a restrictive setting, such as a prison, of which we are members twenty-four hours a day. Goffman said that our appearance can change the way people think about us.

Harlow, Henry (1905–1981) A psychologist who studied the effects of social isolation on rhesus monkeys. Harlow found that monkeys raised in isolation for short periods were able to overcome the effects of their isolation, whereas those isolated more than six months were permanently impaired. Harlow also found mother-child love in monkeys was due to cuddling, not feeding.

Harrington, Michael (1928–1989) A sociologist who argued that colonialism was replaced by neocolonialism. Harrington believed that most industrialized nations tend to exploit less developed countries politically and economically.

Hirschi, Travis (1935–) A sociologist who elaborated on the control theory of deviance and identified four elements that he believed would render an individual more or less likely to commit acts of deviance.

Janis, Irving (1918–1990) The sociologist who coined the term groupthink. Janis used groupthink to describe a phenomenon wherein individuals in positions of power cave in to pressure to agree with the rest of their group until there is only one possible course of action to take.

Lemert, Edwin (1912–1996) The sociologist who differentiated between primary deviance and secondary deviance. Lemert contended that the difference between primary deviance and secondary deviance is in the reactions that other people have to the original act of deviance.

Lewis, Oscar (1914–1970) A social economist who coined the term *culture of poverty*. Lewis maintained that poor people do not learn the norms and values that can help them improve their circumstances and become locked in a cycle of poverty.

Liazos, Alexander (1941–) A sociologist who analyzed the relationship between deviance and power. Liazos concluded that the people most likely to be labeled as deviant were those who were relatively powerless.

Marx, Karl (1818–1883) A German philosopher and social scientist who saw the economy as the key institution in society. Marx felt that workers in a capitalist society are exploited by their employers, and that the capitalist class passes laws to benefit themselves. His books *The Communist Manifesto* and *Capital* spurred the Russian Revolution of 1917.

Mead, George Herbert (1863–1931) A sociologist who believed that people develop their self-images through their interactions with other people. Mead said that the self consists of two parts: the "I" and the "Me." The "I" initiates action. The "Me" continues, interrupts, or changes action depending on others' reactions.

Merton, Robert K. (1910–2003) The sociologist who developed the strain theory of deviance. Merton identified the five ways in which people relate to their cultural goals and the institutionalized means they are given to reach them.

Michels, Robert (1876–1936) A sociologist who developed the theory that bureaucracies are run by a small group of very powerful people who act primarily out of self-interest and actively keep outsiders out. Michels coined the phrase *the iron law of oligarchy.*

Mills, C. Wright (1916–1962) The sociologist who coined the term *power elite.* Mills used power elite to describe a situation in which a nation is run by a few people with the most money and power, rather than by the mass of people.

Ogburn, William (1886–1959) A sociologist who coined the popular term *culture lag,* which refers to the tendency of changes in nonmaterial culture to happen more slowly than those in material culture. In other words, changes in technology eventually bring about later changes in culture.

Piaget, Jean (1896–1980) A pioneer in the field of child psychology. Piaget argued that children develop their thinking capacity in stages and that the progression through these stages depends on a genetically determined timetable. His research changed the way people viewed education, inspiring educators to see that children explore the world actively and come up with their own hypotheses about what they observe.

Reckless, Walter (1898–1988) The sociologist who developed the control theory of deviance. Reckless explored how inner and outer controls could prevent a person from committing deviant acts.

Simmel, Georg (1858–1918) A sociologist who explored the ways in which the size of a group affects its stability and the relationships among its members. Simmel hypothesized that as a group grows larger, its stability increases but its intimacy decreases.

Sutherland, Edwin (1883–1950) The sociologist who developed the theory of differential association. Sutherland asserted that people learn deviance from other people, rather than being biologically predisposed to it.

Thomas, W. I. (1863–1947) A sociologist who analyzed how people use their backgrounds and beliefs about the world to construct their own versions of reality. His Thomas Theorem posits that when a situation is considered real, then its consequences are real.

Tönnies, Ferdinand (1855–1937) A sociologist who developed the theories of *Gemeinschaft*, in which societies are small and intimate and based on close kinship, and *Gesellschaft*, which refers to societies that are large and impersonal and based mainly on self-interest.

Tumin, Melvin (1919–1994) A sociologist who believed that factors other than merit alone determined the type of jobs that people were likely to hold. Tumin believed that social stratification benefits some more than others.

Wallerstein, Immanuel (1930–) The creator of the world system theory, which explains how the globalization of capitalism led to changing relations between countries. Wallerstein said that as capitalism spread, countries around the world became connected to one another in ways they had not been before.

Weber, Max (1864–1920) An economist and sociologist who theorized that religion, not economics, was the central force in social change. He argued that Protestants seeking outward affirmation of their godliness brought about the birth of capitalism. Weber also identified power, the ability to achieve ends even in the face of resistance, as the foundation of government. He named rationality as the key differentiator between non-industrialized and industrialized societies.

Wilson, William Julius (1935–) A social economist who believes that the high level of poverty in the inner cities is due to the lack of jobs. He argues that companies and factories are moving to suburban areas or are outsourcing their labor to foreign countries, decreasing work opportunities available to those in the inner cities and contributing to poverty in those areas.

Glossary

A

Absolute monarchy A political system under which a king or queen has complete control of a country.

Achieved status A status that we either earn or choose and that is not subject to where or to whom we were born.

Agents of socialization People, groups, and experiences that influence our behavior and self-image.

Aggregate A collection of people who happen to be at the same place at the same time but have no other connection to one another.

Agricultural or agrarian society A society that raises crops by using animal-drawn plows.

Alienation The feeling of workers in a bureaucracy that they are being treated as objects rather than people.

American Dream The belief that all Americans, regardless of the conditions of their birth, have an equal chance to achieve success.

Anomie According to strain theory, the feeling of being disconnected from society that can occur when people aren't provided with the institutionalized means to achieve their goals. The term was coined by Émile Durkheim.

Anticipatory socialization The learning of new norms and values in anticipation of a future role.

Apartheid A social system in which there is total separation of the races.

Appearance The way we look physically to other people.

Ascribed status A trait or characteristic people possess as a result of the circumstances of birth.

Assimilation The process whereby members of a group give up parts of their own culture in order to blend in to a new culture.

Authoritarianism A political system that does not allow citizens to participate in government.

B

Belief A specific idea that people feel to be true.

Blue-collar Another term for the *working class*.

Body language The ways in which we use our bodies consciously and unconsciously to communicate.

Bourgeoisie Karl Marx's term for the owners of the means of production—factories, businesses, and equipment needed to produce wealth.

Bureaucracy According to Weber, a type of formal organization in which a rational approach is used for the handling of large tasks.

C

Capitalism The economic system in which the means of production are owned privately and individuals are free to keep the profits they make.

Capitalist class In industrialized societies, the rich and powerful and the owners of the means of production. It is also called the *elite*.

Caste system A system of stratification based on ascribed statuses.

Category A collection of people who share a particular characteristic but have nothing else in common.

Charismatic authority Authority that depends on the personal magnetism of one person, according to Weber's power theory.

Church A religious group integrated with society.

Class system A system of stratification based on achieved statuses.

Clergy The middle stratum of the estate system of stratification, composed of Roman Catholic priests.

Clique An internal cluster or faction within a group.

Colonialism The tendency for a powerful country to invade a weaker country in order to exploit its resources by making it a colony.

Commoners The lowest stratum of the estate system of stratification, composed of the masses of people who spent their lives engaged in hard physical labor.

Communism An economic system similar to socialism in which all the means of production would be owned by everyone and all profits would be shared equally by everyone.

Conflict theory Marx's theory that in any capitalist society there is eternal conflict between the owners of the means of production and the workers.

Conflict view of deviance The view that purports that equality in a capitalist society is an illusion. The owners of the means of production have a vested interest in maintaining the status quo by keeping the working class in a disadvantaged position.

Conformists According to Merton's theory of goals and means, those who accept cultural goals and the institutionalized means of achieving them.

Constitutional monarchy A monarchy in which the reigning member of the royal family is the symbolic head of state but elected officials actually do the governing.

Control theory Walter Reckless's theory that posits that when a person is tempted to engage in deviance, inner controls and outer controls can prevent him or her from doing so.

Counterculture A way of living that opposes the dominant culture.

Crime The violation of a written law.

Crime against the person An act of violence either threatened or perpetrated against a person.

Crime against property The theft of property or certain forms of damage against the property of another person.

Cult A religious group that is outside standard cultural norms.

Cultural diffusion The process whereby an aspect of culture spreads throughout a culture or from one culture to another.

GLOSSARY

Cultural relativism The attitude that in order to understand the traits of another culture, one must view them within the context of that culture.

Culture Everything made, learned, and shared by the members of a society.

Culture lag The tendency for changes in material culture to occur at a more rapid rate than changes in nonmaterial culture.

Culture of poverty The phrase that Oscar Lewis used to describe the idea that poor people do not learn the norms and values that can help them improve their circumstances and hence get trapped in a repeated pattern of poverty.

Culture shock The surprise, disorientation, and fear people can experience upon encountering a different culture.

D

Degradation ceremony Garfinkel's term for the process whereby an individual with a spoiled identity is expelled from a group and stripped of his or her group membership.

Democracy A political system in which citizens periodically choose officials to run their government.

Deviance The violation of a norm.

Deviant subculture A way of living that differs from the dominant culture, in which members share a particular form of deviance.

Differential association Edwin Sutherland's theory that posits that deviance is learned behavior.

Divine right of kings An ideology developed by the nobility during the Middle Ages that posited that the authority of the nobility came directly from God.

Dominant culture The culture held by the majority and/or by the most powerful group in a society.

Dramaturgy Goffman's theory that life is like a never-ending play in which people are actors.

Dyad A group composed of two people.

E

Economy The institution responsible for the production and distribution of goods and services.

Education The institution responsible for preparing young people for a functional place in adult life and for transmitting culture from one generation to the next.

Ego According to Freud, the part of the mind that resolves conflicts between the id and the superego.

Endogamy Marriage between members of the same category, class, or group.

Estate system The three-tiered stratification system used during the Middle Ages.

Ethnocentrism The tendency to judge another culture by the standards of one's own culture.

Ethnomethodology A theoretical perspective formulated by Garfinkel that examines how people's background assumptions help them make sense of everyday situations.

Exogamy Marriage between members of different categories, classes, or groups.

Extended family Several generations or branches of a family.

F

Family The institution responsible for the rearing of children.

Feminization of poverty The phrase that describes the increasing number of female-headed households living at or below the poverty level.

Folkway A norm followed out of convenience or tradition.

Formal organization A secondary group that is organized to achieve specific goals and tends to be large and impersonal.

G

Gender role A set of behaviors, attitudes, and personality characteristics expected and encouraged of a person based on his or her sex.

Gender socialization The tendency for boys and girls to be socialized differently.

Generalized other George Herbert Mead's term for the internalization of the norms and values of a culture.

Global stratification The stratification of nations.

Globalization of capitalism The adoption of capitalism by countries around the world.

Goal displacement A formal organization's displacement of one goal with another in order to continue to exist. It is also called *goal replacement*.

Goals and means Robert Merton's theory that examines how members of a society adapt their goals to the means that society provides of achieving them.

Government The institution responsible for making and enforcing the rules of society and for regulating relations with other societies.

Group Two or more people who interact over time, have a sense of identity or belonging, and have norms that nonmembers do not have.

Group dynamics A term that implies that our thoughts and behavior are influenced by the groups of which we are members and, in turn, we influence the thought process and behavior of the group as a whole.

Groupthink A term coined by Irving Janis that refers to the tendency of people in positions of power to follow the opinions of the group, to the point that there is a narrow view of the issue at hand.

H

Halo effect The assumption that a physically attractive person also possesses other good qualities.

Health The well-being of people.

Holistic medicine A medical approach that involves learning about a patient's physical environment and mental state.

Horticultural society A society in which hand tools are used to grow crops.

Hunting and gathering society A society in which people acquire food by hunting game and gathering edible plants.

I

Id According to Freud, the first part of the mind to develop and the part of the self responsible for the satisfaction of physical states.

Ideal type Max Weber's theoretical model of how a formal organization should function.

Ideology A set of values that people devise to rationalize a particular social custom.

Illegitimate opportunity structures Cloward and Ohlin's term for opportunities for crimes that are a basic part of our society.

Impression management Goffman's term for the tendency of individuals to manipulate the impressions that others have of them.

In-group A group to which one belongs and to which one feels loyalty.

Indentured servitude A system of stratification in which an individual agrees to sell his or her body or labor to another for a specified period of time.

Industrial society A society that uses advanced sources of energy, rather than humans and animals, to run large machinery.

Industrializing nations Countries that are in the process of becoming industrialized; includes most of the countries of the former Soviet Union.

Inner controls According to control theory, the thought processes such as morality or a conscience that reside within people and that can prevent them from committing acts of deviance.

Innovators According to Robert Merton's theory of goals and means, those who accept cultural goals but reject the institutional means of achieving them.

Institution A set of norms surrounding the carrying out of a function necessary for the survival of a society.

Institutionalized means Legitimate, socially approved ways that societies offer their members to achieve culturally approved goals.

L

Labeling theory A theory of deviance put forth by Howard Becker that claims that deviance is that which is so labeled.

Law A norm that is written down and enforced by an official agency.

Least industrialized nations Primarily agricultural nations that account for half of the land on Earth.

Looking-glass self Charles Horton Cooley's theory of socialization, which posits that we form our self-images on the basis of what we perceive to be others' views of us.

M

Macrosociology Sociological analysis focused on large-scale social forces.

Manner of interacting The attitudes that we convey in an attempt to get others to form certain impressions about us. According to Goffman, it is one of the sign vehicles we use to present ourselves to others, along with the setting and our appearance.

Mass media Communications media that direct messages and entertainment at a wide audience.

Mass society A large impersonal society in which individual achievement is valued over kinship ties and in which people often feel isolated from one another.

Master status A status we possess that overrides all other statuses and becomes the one by which we are known to others.

Material culture The tangible, visible items of a culture.

Matrilocality A social custom in which married couples live in the home of the wife's family.

Medicine The institution responsible for defining and treating mental and physical problems among its members.

Melting pot A term used to refer to a pluralistic society in which people who originally come from different societies blend together to form a new society.

Meritocracy A system of stratification in which positions are given according to individual merit.

Microsociology Sociological analysis focused on social interaction between individuals.

Middle class The class that consists of people who earn their money by working at professional jobs, also called *white-collar* jobs.

Monarchy A political system in which a representative from one family controls the government and power is passed on through that family from generation to generation.

Monogamy Marriage between one man and one woman.

Monotheism Belief in a single deity.

Moral reasoning The reasons that people think the way they do about what's right and wrong.

More A norm based on notions of morality.

Most industrialized nations Highly industrialized, capitalistic countries, including America, Canada, Great Britain, France, Germany, and Japan.

Multiculturalism A term often used instead of "melting pot" to denote a pluralistic society in which the original cultural heritages of its citizens are recognized and respected.

Multinational corporations Large corporations that do business in a number of different countries.

N

Negative sanction A socially constructed expression of disapproval.

Neocolonialism Michael Harrington's term for the tendency of the most industrialized nations to exploit less developed countries politically and economically.

Neolocality A social custom in which married couples move to a new home of their own together.

Network A series of social ties that can be important sources of information, contacts, and assistance for its members.

New money The class that consists of people whose wealth has been around only for a generation or two.

Nobility The highest stratum of the estate system of stratification. Members had significant inherited wealth and did little or no discernible work.

Nonmaterial culture The intangible, invisible parts of a culture, such as values.

Norm A guideline or an expectation for behavior.

Nuclear family One or both parents and their children.

O

Oligarchy The rule of the many by the few.

Out-group A group to which one does not belong and to which one does not feel loyalty.

Outer controls According to control theory, individuals who encourage people not to stray into deviance.

P

Pastoral society A society that relies on the domestication and breeding of animals for food.

Patrilocality A social custom in which married couples live in the home of the husband's family.

Peer group A social group in which members are usually the same age and have interests and social position in common.

Personal space The area immediately around one's body that one can claim as one's own.

Pluralistic society A society composed of many different kinds of people.

Polyandry Marriage between one woman and more than one man.

Polygamy Marriage between one man and more than one woman.

Polytheism Belief in many deities.

Positive sanction A socially constructed expression of approval.

Postindustrial society A society that features an economy based on services and technology, not production.

Poverty level An estimate set by the federal government of the minimum income that a family of four needs to survive.

Power According to Weber, the ability to achieve ends even in the face of resistance.

Power elite A term coined by C. Wright Mills that refers to his theory that the United States is actually run by a small group representing the most wealthy, powerful, and influential people in business, government, and the military.

Primary deviance According to Lemert, a deviant act that elicits little or no reaction from others.

Primary group A group in which there is frequent face-to-face contact, little task orientation, and emotional intimacy among members.

Primary socialization The learning that we experience from the people who raise us.

Primogeniture A law stipulating that only a first-born son could inherit his father's wealth.

Proletariat Karl Marx's term for the working masses.

Props The things used to decorate a setting, according to Goffman's theory of impression management. Props also include manner of dress.

R

Rational-legal authority Authority that rests on rules and laws, according to Weber's power theory.

Rationalization of society Weber's theory that bureaucracies would gain increasing power over modern life, eventually governing almost every aspect of society.

Rebels According to Robert Merton's theory of goals and means, those who reject both cultural goals and the institutionalized means of achieving them, but who replace them with goals and means of their own.

Recidivism The tendency of convicted criminals to repeat offenses.

Reference group The group to whom we compare ourselves for purposes of self-evaluation.

Reincarnation The belief that while the physical body dies, the soul of a person is immortal and goes on to be reborn into another body.

Religion The institution responsible for answering people's larger questions and for explaining the seemingly inexplicable.

Resocialization The learning of new norms and values.

Retreatists According to Robert Merton's theory of goals and means, those who reject cultural goals as well as the institutionalized means of achieving them.

Revolution A violent overthrow of the government by its citizens.

Ritualists According to Robert Merton's theory of goals and means, those who reject cultural goals but accept the institutionalized means of achieving them.

Role A set of norms, values, and personality characteristics expected of a person based on the setting he or she is in.

Role conflict The conflict that can result from the competing demands of two or more roles.

S

Sanction A socially constructed expression of approval or disapproval.

Secondary deviance According to Lemert, repeated deviant behavior that is brought on by other people's negative reactions to the original act of deviance.

Secondary group A group in which there is infrequent or short-term contact, little task orientation, and no emotional intimacy among members.

Sect A religious group that sets itself apart from society as a whole.

Self The part of a person's personality consisting of self-awareness and self-image.

Setting The place where interaction takes place. According to Goffman, it is one of the sign vehicles we use to present ourselves to others, along with manner of interacting and appearance.

Sign vehicles Goffman's term for the mechanisms we use to present ourselves to others. Sign vehicles consist of setting, appearance, and manner of interacting.

Significant other According to Charles Horton Cooley, a person in our lives whose opinions matter to us and who is in a position to influence our thinking.

Skilled worker A worker who is literate and has experience and expertise in specific areas of production or on specific kinds of machines.

Slavery A system of stratification in which one person owns another, usually for economic gain.

Social control The ways a society devises to encourage conformity to norms.

Social construction of reality A theory suggesting that the way in which we present ourselves is shaped by our life experiences, as well as by our interactions with others.

Social group Two or more people who interact and identify with each other.

Social integration The degree to which an individual feels connected to the other people in his or her group or community.

Social mobility Movement up or down the social hierarchy.

Society's rewards The things a society holds in high esteem, such as wealth, power, and prestige.

Socialism A system under which resources and means of production are owned by the society as a whole, rights to private property are limited, the good of the whole society is stressed more than individual profit, and the government maintains control of the economy.

Socialization The process whereby we learn to become competent members of a group.

Society A collection of people with territory, interaction, and a culture.

Socioeconomic status (SES) A calculation based on a complex formula that takes into account education, occupation, and income.

Spoiled identity Goffman's term for an identity that has been permanently ruined because of a severe stigma.

State capitalism A system under which resources and means of production are privately owned but closely monitored and regulated by the government.

Status The position that a person occupies in a particular setting.

Status inconsistency Any inconsistency between various statuses.

Status set The collection of all of our different statuses, from every setting in which we are a member.

Status symbol A sign or symbol that we wear or carry that represents a particular status.

Stereotype An assumption we make about a person or a group, often on the basis of incorrect or incomplete information.

Stigma Goffman's term for a trait that we possess that causes us to lose prestige in the eyes of others.

Strain theory Robert Merton's theory that posits that people experience strain and frustration when they are prevented from achieving culturally approved goals through institutionalized means.

Stratification A societal system in which there is an unequal distribution of society's rewards and in which people are arranged hierarchically into layers according to how many of society's rewards they possess.

Structural functionalist theory A sociological view of society as a complex unit made up of interrelated parts. Sociologists who apply this theory study social structure and social function.

Subculture A group that espouses a way of living that is different from that of the dominant culture.

Superego According to Freud, the part of the mind that encourages conformity to societal norms and values. It is also called the conscience.

Symbolic interactionist perspective A sociological framework that views society as a product of the everyday social interactions of individuals.

T

Taboo A norm so strongly held by a society that its violation brings extreme disgust.

Terrorism A politically motivated violent attack on civilians by an individual or group.

Thomas Theorem The theory espousing sociologist W. I. Thomas's idea that "if a person perceives a situation as real, it is real in its consequences."

Total institution According to Erving Goffman, a highly standardized institution in which all the residents' actions are determined and monitored by authority figures.

Totalitarianism A political system under which the government maintains tight control over nearly all aspects of citizens' lives.

Traditional authority Authority that rests on well-established cultural patterns, according to Weber's power theory.

Triad According to Georg Simmel, a group composed of three people.

U

Upper class The highest social group, consisting of people with inherited wealth and a recognizable family name.

Urbanization The process by which the majority of a population comes to live within commuting distance of a major city.

V

Value A culturally approved belief about what is right or wrong, desirable or undesirable.

Victimless crime Crimes in which laws are violated but there is no identifiable victim.

Voluntary association A group we choose to join, in which members are united by the pursuit of a common goal.

W

War Armed conflict between nations or societies.

Welfare capitalism A system that features a market-based economy coupled with an extensive social welfare system that includes free health care and education for all citizens.

White collar Middle-class workers; so called because of the tendency of middle-class men to wear white shirts to work.

White-collar crime Nonviolent crime committed by the capitalist class during the course of their occupations.

Working class The class composed of people who sell their labor to a higher class. They may have had vocational or technical training and have jobs such as electrician or factory worker.

Working poor The class composed of people whose work leaves them vulnerable to falling below the poverty level.

World system theory Wallerstein's theory that as societies industrialized, capitalism became the dominant economic system, leading to the globalization of capitalism.

Index

INDEX

INDEX

Slavery, 167–168, 170, 186, 196, 219
  causes of, 167–168
  global history, 167
  in the U.S., 168
Small, Albion, 2
Social behaviorism, Mead's theory of, 43
Social classes, 181–182, 198
  and crime, 153, 162
  middle class, 182
  new money, 181–182
  poverty level, 183
  upper class, 181
  working class, 182–183
  working poor, 183
Social construction of life stages, 51
Social construction of reality, 118–119, 134, 220
  ethnomethodology, 119
  Thomas Theorem, 119
Social controls, 20, 39, 139–140, 160, 220
Social groups, 8, 91–116, 220
  aggregates, 92–93
  categories, 93
  group classifications, 93–97
  groups, 92
  social integration, 97–100
Social institutions, 65–90
  economy, 66–67, 88
  education, 79, 90
  family, 73–75
  government, 69–73, 88–89
  medicine, 79–81, 90
  religion, 75–78, 89–90
Social integration, 97–100, 115, 220
  Durkheim's study of suicide, 97–98
  group dynamics, 98–99
  group size/member interaction, 99–100
Social isolation, 49–50
Social mobility, 173, 197, 220
Social pressure, 100
Social sciences, 3–4
Social setting, 120–121

Social status, 124–127, 135
  degradation ceremonies, 126–127
  and deviance, 139, 160
  master status, 125
  status inconsistency, 124–125
  status symbols, 124
  stigmas, 125–126
Social stratification, 176
  and agricultural societies, 164–165
  categories, historical stratification systems, 196
  functionalist perspective, 175–176
  historical stratification systems, 167–169
  and horticultural societies, 164–165
  hunting and gathering societies, 164
  industrialization, 165–166
  modern stratification systems, 170–173, 197
  origins of, 164–166, 196
  postindustrial societies, 166
  poverty in America, 184–186
  stratification system of the U.S., 177–180
  theories of, 174–176, 197
  in the U.S., 197
Social welfare, and sociologists, 5
Socialism, 67, 88, 220
  capitalism vs., 67
Socialization, 41–61, 62, 220
  anticipatory, 53, 63, 207
  defined, 42
  gender, 53–55, 63
  as a lifelong learning process, 56
  primary, 42–52
  resocialization, 50–52
Societies, 38, 220
  defined, 7
  origin of term, 7
  types of, 12–13, 38
Society's rewards, 220
Socioeconomic status (SES), 177–180, 181, 198, 220
  education, 177–178
  income, 180–181
  occupation, 179–180
Sociologists, role of, 4–5

INDEX

INDEX